CH

COULDN'T
HOLD ME

CHAINS COULDN'T HOLD ME

CEDRIC FISHER

LIGHTHOUSE TRAILS PUBLISHING
EUREKA, MONTANA

Library of Congress Cataloging-in-Publication Data

Names: Fisher, Cedric, 1949- author.
Title: Chains couldn't hold me / Cedric Fisher.
Description: 1st Edition. | Eureka : Lighthouse Trails Publishing, 2018.
Identifiers: LCCN 2018007782 | ISBN 9781942423317 (softbound : alk. paper)
Subjects: LCSH: Fisher, Cedric, 1949- | Clergy--United States--Biography. |
  Christian biography--United States.
Classification: LCC BR1725.F495 A3 2018 | DDC 277.3/083092 [B]
--dc23 LC record available at https://lccn.loc.gov/2018007782

Printed in the United States of America

To Cheryl,
my wife, great listener, advisor,
and forever best friend

CONTENTS

Then they cried unto the Lord in their trouble,

And He saved them out of their distresses.

He brought them out of darkness

and the shadow of death,

And broke their [chains] in sunder.

—Psalm 107:13-14

The relentless summer sun of 1951 blistered the landscape in the flat, dry counties of southern Oklahoma. It was so hot that the trees bowed their heads. Even wildlife took shelter from the inferno that scorched the grass into a pale khaki. One would not expect to see anyone on foot that time of day. But there they were—walking beside the concrete ribbon called US Highway 69. In the distance, fading in and out of the shimmering dance of the heat waves, a man, woman, and three young boys trudged along in the furnace. What were they doing in a place even the most educated Okie would label, "Out in the middle of nowhere"? The story of who they were and how they got there is not nearly as complex as the story of the youngest boy. That boy was me—Cedric Hamilton Fisher.

CHAPTER 1

TRANSIENT FAMILY

I was born poor, "dirt poor," as they say where I came from. Born in Dallas, Texas, the third son of Samuel Aubrey and Christine Fisher, I didn't get to stay long enough to get Texas in my blood. Like many other nomadic, poor, post-depression families, Mama and Dad followed the jobs. From the stories Mama told, Dad had worked at jobs in Oklahoma, Arkansas, Missouri, and Texas. He either quit, was fired, or the jobs simply ran out. Consequently, we often had little or no money, never decent homes, and were perpetually hungry.

However, to present the full picture, I must back up to the time Mama and Dad began their lives together. Their story took root on February 27, 1943, the day Mama and Dad were married in Arkansas. In September of the same year, they moved to Dallas, Texas. Dad had heard there were plenty of jobs available in that area. Their arrival in Dallas had an inglorious beginning. Home was an old dilapidated rental shack in a slum neighborhood. They would have fled that seedy domicile after the first week, but their jobs didn't pay enough for them to relocate outside the impoverished and crime-ridden area.

Eventually, they saved enough to move into a small apartment. However, their troubles piled up like rubble in the Dallas gutters. Dad became sick with the flu shortly after the move and quit working. Mama was three-months pregnant, had morning sickness, and could not eat or drink without becoming nauseated, but she continued working. After becoming ill with the same sickness, she continued working until she was so weak she became bedridden. Dad reluctantly went back to work.

Taken not long after Mama and
Dad were married. Probably the
happiest she ever was with him.

After a doctor visit, the doctor shook his finger in Dad's face and told him to take care of his wife. He cooked her breakfast the next morning, and that was the extent of his caretaking. When he got home that afternoon, he coldly told her, " You'd better get up or you'll forget how to walk." He refused to do anything more for her.

I do not know what kept Mama from packing up and leaving Dad and Dallas in the smoke of a Greyhound bus, but she stayed and fought to make her one-sided marriage work. Amazingly, she recovered and went back to her job until she was five months pregnant. At that point, the doctor told her to quit, or she would lose the baby. Dad became furious when she quit, and he only worked sporadically. When Grandma Barnes came to care for Mama until the baby was born, Dad refused to work the entire two weeks she was there.

In spite of the hardships Mama endured, my oldest brother, Charles, was born at noon on Saturday, July 29, 1944.

Dad reluctantly went back to work, and they moved into an apartment. However, he took a night job, which required him to sleep during the day. He insisted Mama maintain complete silence during his sleeping hours. There was immeasurable stress on her to keep the baby quiet in a small apartment. One day, Charles, four months old at the time, began crying. Dad was not sleeping at the moment but was writing a song. He cursed and demanded that Mama silence Charles. No matter what she tried, she couldn't get the baby to stop crying. He was probably hungry, and there was seldom anything for him to eat. She describes what occurred in her memoir:

"Aubrey came rushing over, put his hands around my throat and started choking me. I couldn't scream because my breath was being squeezed off. He stopped before I collapsed, then ran out of the house, afraid I would call the law, but I didn't."

After that bizarre incident, Dad refused to go back to work, so Mama became employed as a common laborer in building construction in order to feed the family. Dad agreed to take care of Charles and maintain the house while she was at work. She came home the first evening to discover that Charles had been shut up in the kitchen all day without food or water. The kitchen was a mess with broken glass and food pulled out of the refrigerator. Mama bitterly complained but came home to the same scenario every day. With Dad on a lazy strike and Mama's income insufficient to survive on, they decided to leave Dallas. So they packed up and moved in with Mama's family in Warren, Arkansas.

Seven months later, they moved from Arkansas to Saint Louis, Missouri. One night, Mama was sitting in a chair embroidering. She was seven months pregnant with her second son, Clarence. Charles was asleep, and all was quiet. She was startled when without warning Dad came at her with a hammer. Mama thought she was going to die that night. She wrote in her memoir, "I thought my time had come. Aubrey came over with a hammer, drew it back like he was going to beat me to death. Don't know what made him do that."

The fact that Dad had gotten a hammer indicates premeditation of intent to murder Mama. He probably had a story concocted that he was convinced would exonerate him of any possibility of guilt. I do not believe that a sense of decency stopped him from going ahead with his plan that night. It is possible he may have lost confidence at the last moment and figured he'd get caught.

Shortly after that terrifying incident, Mama moved with Dad back to Dallas, Texas. They walked all day long through the slum neighborhoods looking for a rental. Charles was two years old, and Mama was nearly full-term pregnant with Clarence. Eventually, they found a one-room flop shack that rented for $5 per week. Mama described it as a small decrepit one room with two beds, an old trunk, a large wooden box, an old cabinet, one chair, and a cook stove. My next-to-the-oldest brother, Clarence, was born during that period. He was brought home to the squalor of that accommodation.

Charles was two years and Clarence was eight months old when the landlord, without notice, raised the rent on the shack. Dad angrily refused to pay the increase. He complained to the landlord that there had been no improvements to the ramshackle shanty and its unsanitary condition. Mama relates what happened later in her memoir:

"They came over one night, we thought to visit. Aubrey opened the door; they ask him to come out, so he did, and both jumped on him and pistol whipped him. The law came but didn't do anything with them. Aubrey sued them and got over $200.00."

After that episode, they moved from the shack into a better dwelling, but a worse situation. Mama described it as "hell in force." The family who owned the place frequently argued using loud vulgarity and were often drunk. Dad did not work enough to pay the rent and buy many groceries. Thus, Charles and Clarence seldom had any milk or anything to eat.

It was into that volatile situation I was born. On February 1, 1949, six years after Mama and Dad united in matrimony, I unceremoniously entered the world. There was nothing else written in Mama's memoir about my birth. Fifteen months later, when Mama was six months pregnant with her fourth child, Dad decided they should again leave Dallas and move to Muskogee, Oklahoma.

———— ··◁✖▷·· ————

That brings my story back to that summer day in 1951 when our family walked along State Highway 69 in the sweltering heat typical of Texas and Oklahoma summers. I wonder what drove my Dad to put his family at such an extreme risk. Maybe it was foolhardy determination. Considering his other random and inexplicable antics, it may have been a genuine mental issue. However, I wonder more about why Mama would follow such a man. Nonetheless, she tackled the challenge with unreserved commitment.

There were numerous dangers a man and woman with three small children could encounter making such a journey. America was not that far down the road from the Great Depression. The poor were the last to recover—if they ever did in that generation.

Some people would do almost anything to survive. Stories had circulated about people driving down highways and seeing a purse lying on the side of the road. When they stopped to investigate, thugs would leap out of the bushes, then beat and rob them.

Dad led us down State Highway 69, no doubt hoping not to be caught on it after dark. He tried to hitch a ride for us, but no one would stop. Throughout the day, he fumed and ranted at passing vehicles that could have accommodated our family. It is approximately 235 miles from Dallas, Texas to Muskogee, Oklahoma—a near impossible journey on foot with children. Additionally, we did not have enough money to spend the night in a room along the way.

I do not recall a great deal about that event. I seem to remember being very hungry, tired, and thirsty, but not much more. Nevertheless, to this day, I have dreams of struggling in traumatic or hostile scenarios. Perhaps they come from the stress of frequently moving during the first few years of my life. Maybe these dreams stem from the trauma of harsh events occurring after we finally settled down. Maybe it is some of both. The only reliable information from that period comes from Mama's memoir:

"We started out hitchhiking—three little boys, plus one on the way, three months to go. We caught the bus somewhere on the way to Durant, Okla. We sat up that night in the bus station. We ate pancakes for breakfast that morning and started hitchhiking again. We got very few rides on the way—but we walked 34 miles that day. I being six months pregnant carrying a fifteen-month-old boy—leading a three year old by the hand and keeping the five year old on the side of the highway.

"My heels had blisters on them the size of my heels: little Clarence would say, Mama I can't walk any more, and he and Charles would sit down and rest. Aubrey was carrying two bags of a change of clothes for the five of us.

"The boys got rested, and we tarried on down the highway toward Muskogee. We finally caught a 100-mile ride that brought us into Muskogee.

"We sat up in the bus station that night. The next morning, we started out again. Hitchhiking to his mother's, which was at Texanna, Oklahoma around 10-15 miles. [Actually, it is about 39 miles.] We caught a ride with some school teacher that taught school within a mile of Aubrey's mother's home. But he had her let us off about four miles before we got to his mother's home. He guided us through the woods that four miles. My heels were so sore, and we got scratched up, the boys and I."

In spite of the formidable odds, we somehow made it to Grandma Carrie's house in Texanna, Oklahoma. Grandpa Samuel had died some year prior, and she had remarried. Her second husband had also died, so she lived alone when we arrived at her house. However, we didn't stay very long at Grandma Carrie's house. The day after we arrived, Dad headed back to Muskogee to find a job. He found one mowing lawns and managed to rent an apartment on credit, albeit in the worst part of town. Then he hitchhiked back to Texanna to get us. The following day, the whole family hitchhiked and walked to our apartment in Muskogee.

During that period in Muskogee, Mama gave birth to a baby girl,

Mama and Dad

19

Nancy. Shortly after, Dad's lawn mowing work ended, and he could not find a steady job. Unable to pay rent, we lived primarily on charity from a church. Six weeks after Nancy was born, Dad decided we should move to Arkansas. So we shipped some of our belongings, hitchhiked, and rode to Fort Smith, Arkansas.

Fort Smith changed nothing about our situation but the geography. Dad initially got a job at a drive-in burger restaurant, but we did not have a place to live. He had found a two-room apartment, but he did not like it. He quit the drive-in job after one day and got a job digging ditches. Homeless for five days, we wandered about looking for another place to live. We spent our nights in the Frisco Railroad station. During the day, Mama took us to the park. She bathed us and then washed our clothes while we played with some other children.

On the fifth day, someone must have noticed our emaciated and ragged condition and called the police. Mama was arrested, and we were all brought to the District Attorney's office. After threatening to take us away and put her and Dad in jail if changes were not made, he let us go free. After we were released, Mama went to where Dad was working and told him what had occurred. He was enraged and wanted to retaliate against the District Attorney. He wrote in his memoir:

"Nothing would have pleased me more than a chance to cut that D.A.'s throat with my knife. For the first time in my life, I had a real impulse to commit murder. To this day, I hate the name Fort Smith and think less of the voters who elected such an unscrupulous and stupid man to serve as their District Attorney."

I believe Dad was capable of doing what he wrote. Later in life, I met a guy who told me Dad had killed a man during a fit of rage. For some reason unknown to me, he was not sent to prison.

It is likely Dad inherited his unbridled temper from his father. One time, his Dad, Samuel William Fisher (whom I never met), could not get all his mules to enter the feedlot. In a rage and spouting vulgarity, Grandpa Samuel went in the house, came back with his rifle, and shot dead the stubborn ones.

Grandma Carrie told us that on another occasion, Grandpa Samuel sent her to fetch a bucket of drinking water. When she returned, his half-wit friend spat a stream of tobacco juice in the water as she was passing by. She set it down in front of my Grandpa Samuel, and he became furious. He ordered her to bring another bucket of water. She refused on the basis of what his friend had done. Grandpa Samuel picked up a stick of firewood and threw it, hitting her in the head and knocking her unconscious. Grandma Carrie lay on the floor in a puddle of blood for a long period. When she regained consciousness, he growled,

My dad's father, Samuel William Fisher, who nearly killed my Grandma Carrie

"Now go get that bucket of water like I said."

I am ashamed to have the genes of such a man in my blood. Mama and us kids visited Grandma Carrie often before she died. She was a sweet and loving lady who outlived her poor excuse for a husband. It was difficult to believe that any

Grandma Carrie was part Muscogee Indian. A photo of her as a young woman.

man could treat her or another human with such contempt and brutality. I am glad I never met him and that he was not around when we lived briefly with Grandma Carrie in Texanna, Oklahoma.

Dad quit his ditch-digging job, and we somehow slept that first night in the apartment he initially refused to move into. He must have picked the lock or otherwise found a way inside. Perhaps we could have had a place to live on the first day, but he chose not to spend the money. Nonetheless, the next day, we moved into a one-room apartment near Van Buren across the river from Fort Smith. A short time later, Dad was hired at a waste-paper plant.

A month later, the waste-paper plant caught fire, and Dad was again without a job. He refused to look for another job and decided we should move to Mama's parent's home. Mama was pregnant for the fifth time. She did not want to move back in with her parents, but Dad insisted. So, again, we moved approximately 245 miles to Warren, Arkansas. I do not know whether we were invited or if Mama and Dad invited themselves. Nonetheless, we moved in with my other grandparents, Grandpa and Grandma Barnes.

Grandpa and Grandma Barnes

It was not a good arrangement. I think we wore out our welcome rather quickly. Benjamin Franklin was quoted as saying, "Fish and visitors stink after three days." That is probably not far from the truth. Grandma's house was not very large, and we had a large family. However, the major issue was Dad's unrestrained temper and vulgarity.

It isn't difficult to understand why Grandma Barnes wanted Dad out of her house. Grandma went to a strict holiness church. She had a no-tolerance policy when it came to vulgarity. Additionally, a bizarre incident may have set the tone for the contention that later developed between Grandma Barnes and Dad. It occurred one evening when some of Mama's siblings came over for a visit. We were all sitting outside, and we were playing with my nephew who was about the same age as my brother Clarence. He was a handsome child with blonde wavy hair.

The little man stood on a stump in the yard preaching. I am certain we had never heard an adult preach like that, much less a young boy. The adults were immensely entertained by his antics. However, he stepped too close to the edge of the stump, fell backward, and his head landed on a large rock.

My aunt and uncle rushed him to the hospital, but he had slipped into a coma. He died a few hours later. The incident brought near intolerable grief into the family. Grandma no doubt suffered greatly because her little grandson had died in her yard. Everyone in the household was in mourning except apparently Dad.

Grandma's tolerance ran out when one day Dad flew into one of his vulgar rages one too many times. The incident occurred shortly after my sister Cathy was born. Mama wrote about the event in her memoir:

"Aubrey didn't go back to work any way soon. He tried his hand at trapping. Every time he would to tend his traps, it would rain—most every time.

"Aubrey was a big cusser. So he started cussing "God" for it raining so much. That was the last straw for my mother. So she got the double barrel shot gun and told him to leave, or she would shoot him."

Dad left immediately and didn't come back. He got odd jobs and lived wherever he could. However, Grandma Barnes' threat must have shocked some sense into him. He sent Mama some money from every paycheck until we had enough to leave Arkansas. I cannot remember if we traveled all the way by bus, hitchhiked and walked, or some of all three. Nonetheless, we arrived for the second time at Grandma Carrie's house in Texanna, Oklahoma.

My cousin, Bobby Dean (the boy preacher), with one of my uncles

Dad departed shortly afterward to find us a place to live in Checotah, Oklahoma. He eventually sent word for us to come, but he didn't send any money to go by bus. So Mama gathered up us boys and the two girls, and we walked sixteen miles to Checotah. Even though by that time, it was apparent Dad was an incurable wanderer and totally irresponsible, Mama remained completely loyal and resolved to follow him.

Many hours after starting out, we arrived in Checotah. Mama began asking directions to the house my Dad had rented. I'll never forget that chance meeting with him. Tired, hungry, dirty, and going

24

on little sleep, we were plodding down a dirt and graveled road toward the rental house. We saw a car racing down the road toward us like a low-flying crop duster—dust churning from the wheels. Just as we thought it would pass by, the car swung over to the side of the road and slid to a stop. Inside, was my Dad and another man.

Hat cocked over to one side and a hand-rolled cigarette dangling out of the corner of his mouth, he did not appear very excited to see us. He chatted briefly with Mama as if they had not been separated for days. I was too young to understand everything they discussed. He never got out of the car, hugged her, or even leaned out the window to kiss her.

One would expect that he would have at least given us a ride to the rental house. Instead, he gave directions. Then, he and his friend sped on their way, fogging us with dust in the process.

They were in a hurry to go somewhere, but I'm fairly certain at that time of day, it was not to a job. Knowing Dad, they were probably headed out to have some fun. I was disappointed and confused. I thought when we met up with him the hard times would be over. Mama complained bitterly about him driving off like that. In my memories, I can hear the pain in her voice.

It seems that Mama and pain were close companions. I remember her tears. I remember her frowning. But I do not remember her laughing. I can't even remember her eyes smiling or glowing with joy. In fact, it would be a long period before I would hear Mama laugh for the first time.

I am not certain Dad ever loved my Mama. He was a charismatic and handsome charmer—able to lure a woman but totally incapable of loving one. His narcissism prevented him from loving anyone but himself. I believe that on the day of that chance encounter, we were an annoyance, an unexpected intrusion in his immediate plan of hanging out with his buddy. I don't believe he expected Mama to walk all the way from Texanna with five children. He was probably as shocked to see us as we were glad to see him.

When Dad left us standing in the dust, we were on the outskirts of what people called "colored town." It was and remains today a poor community across the railroad tracks on the east side of the small city. The last mile of our journey took us all the way through "colored town" past the very end of northeast fifth street. In fact, the house Dad had rented at twenty dollars per month was just outside the city limits.

When we reached the house, we initially felt some relief. It was a medium frame house jutted against the blank canvas of a flat, colorless pasture. With full-length front and back porches and yellow asbestos-cement siding under a red roof, it appeared huge and grand. But it was empty and sorely lacking on the inside. It had no furniture and no appliances. Dad brought into the kitchen and dining area an old rotting table from the yard. He put together some makeshift stools, and that was all we had. Later, he came home with a hotplate for Mama to cook on. Little good it did since there was not much food to cook. Again, Mama tells about the situation in her memoir:

"So there we were—another baby on the way, already had five hungry babies—crying most of the time because they were hungry. When Aubrey did manage to bring in a little food, I'd try to give most of it to the children, but Aubrey would hog it up from them."

Nevertheless, it would be our sometimes-happy and some-times-volatile domicile for nearly a decade. The experiences and memories in that small piece of the world would chisel my purpose in life down to the pursuit of one goal—getting as far away as possible from it all. The force of poverty would birth and develop my obsession of achieving wealth and fame.

CHAPTER 2

POVERTY ROAD

Memories from my early years in Checotah, Oklahoma luminesce with the spectacle of ramshackle houses, bare dirt front yards, our dogs, and black folks sitting on unpainted porches. Those scenes are accompanied by the sounds of life, of crackling radio music, children's voices, and mothers calling out to them. When I recollect those days, I can smell the evenings. Evenings in the neighborhood were flavored by the tantalizing aroma of suppers simmering just beyond open windows and tattered screen doors. If I close my eyes now, my mind swims in odorous delight of the reduction cooking. Oh . . . and the pungent odor of chitlins.

Our neighborhood was by design a society divided by a railroad track from the small town. A tight clique of black families who knew life had pinned them in occupied it. There was no choice but to struggle or get out, go elsewhere, someplace where there were jobs. In the struggling itself, there was necessary innovation to piece together into usability the scraps of existence. Life required it. Those who failed to forcibly make ends meet were consigned to dwell amongst its shambles. It was the simple, predictable, and rustic monotony of poverty. The indomitable and oft repeated motto was, "Somehow we'll make it through."

Then there was the blue funk of the night. It seemed that when night fell, everything died but the dogs. During midday, one would scarcely hear a dog barking. At night, it was a dog concert. As I listened to the dogs barking through our open bedroom windows, I wondered if they were talking to each other or repeatedly warning an evil intruder. I feared the night and didn't like having to go to bed. I wouldn't go into the bedroom without first turning on the light. Evil lurked in the dark, waiting to do something horrible to me.

There were occasions while I was outside when the sun fell behind the trees. Silhouettes of nondescript houses, windows faintly glowing with yellow light, loom in my imaginative mind as a maze one could be drawn into and never come out of. The neighborhood, whose trails, back streets, and inner workings only the inhabitants knew, became intimidating and foreboding in the dark.

But the weekends were different and permeated with more human activity and sounds. The noise of partying on Saturday nights sometimes rode on the soft breezes. Laughter, sometimes arguing, and an occasional gunshot filled the air. Somewhere, deep in the ebony maze, someone would be singing or even playing the blues. There were a couple of bootlegger houses in our neighborhood where one could get a quart of "shine." Maybe they had live music, a radio, or record player.

We seldom had visitors from the neighborhood. Not long after we first arrived, some of the neighborhood children came to check us out. Their curiosity satisfied, the visits dwindled. It was as if an invisible fence existed between our neighbors and us. Although we were poor and struggling like everyone in the community, we were still a white family—the only one in the neighborhood. The short stretch of road between our house and the rest of the community appeared as our driveway. Actually, it was a short L-appendage off the end of northeast fifth street that ended at our gate. The dilapidated old gate was a shambling demarcation keeping us in and our neighbors out. We seldom ventured beyond it.

One of the houses we lived in while growing up

The penalty of poverty was that we had the same daily goals as the wildlife—finding something to eat, someplace to shelter, and staying out of harm's way. Dad worked at odd jobs and foraged for items in the city dump, which he turned around and sold for what he could get. He also appealed to people for food and loans.

We kids remained at home with Mama most of the time. Except for visits to the grocery store and church, our whole world was inside the fenced-in yard. The fact is that we were as poor as the poorest in our community. However, inside of our "gated" compound poverty was somewhat mitigated by the constant activity and commotion.

Five kids, hardwood floors, slamming screen doors, and window fans made poverty wait its turn to be acknowledged.

We had never known wealth or anything resembling it. Thus, the standard by which we judged our existence was very low. We had a dog, Nicky, and several feral cats that lived in one of the barns, and a yard full of chickens. If we played and obeyed, life was uncomplicated and somewhat serene. At the time, I didn't want more because I didn't know there was more. We did not become poor until someone told us we were poor. Maybe they didn't say it in words, but they did with their demeanor or the contrast of their abundant and superior possessions.

L to R: Me, Clarence, Charles, and sister Nancy

We didn't have a TV, so we had no clue how the rest of the world lived. A highlight was when people came to visit. For us kids especially, the excitement of company coming gave us a sense of awe at the newness of our guests. Our house actually faced the west, but everyone came and went through the kitchen and the back door.

The adults sat on the back porch and drank iced tea. Men spat snuff juice and talked about matters over my head. The women chatted about cooking and sewing. I sat on the edge of the porch feeling special because I was allowed to experience such an event.

In April of 1953, less than a year after we arrived at the end of Northeast fifth Street, the youngest girl, Martha, was born. My brother Clarence and I met Mama at the door. We were surprised to see how tiny she was. Her arrival made it a total of six mouths to feed, clothe, shelter, and nurture. Mom managed three out of those four requirements. I honestly cannot fault her for being unable to perform the last one.

Often I didn't understand or pay attention to the activity going on around me. I was alone most of the time and lived in my own small world. My older brothers stuck together and shut me out. The girls didn't have anything to do with me. Except for those grand occasions when we had company, there was not much to do but play in the yard.

The summers were Oklahoma dry, so dry that as one old fellow put it, "The dogs are marking their territory with chalk." Entertainment was chasing butterflies, playing with June bugs on a string, rolling an old tire around, or exploring the old barn. I explored it repeatedly, each time with the expectation I would find something new. I never did. It was the same old rundown and musty-smelling structure. The same "pride" of feral cats ran and dived for a hole in the floor each time I snuck in trying to catch them napping.

Quite possibly, I experienced middle-child syndrome. I had no relationship with Mama. Likewise, Dad was as a stranger to me. He never made an attempt to connect with me. I cannot remember him ever holding me or talking to me. In fact, I cannot remember Mama or Dad ever saying, "I love you." I was in awe of him. He appeared big and threatening. However, Dad favored Clarence. He sometimes took Clarence with him when he went to sell beer and whiskey bottles to the bootleggers.

Dad was a talented songwriter and singer. When he was home, he often practiced his singing. But it was not to entertain us; life was all about him. He often became agitated when our noise distracted him. He'd stomp through the house fuming and railing. I knew to get out of the way of his feet. Dad frequented the bars and nightclubs where he could chum with his friends, sing, and entertain people. When he or his buddies ran out of money, or there was nothing more exciting to do, he came home. He treated Mama more like a slave than a wife.

A memory etched in my mind is of standing beside Mama as she hovered over the sink. She was washing whiskey bottles for Dad to sell to bootleggers. I looked up at her anxious face. I can hear her voice breaking as tears flowed down her cheeks and into the suds.

Mama and Dad

Farther along we'll know all about it.
Farther along we'll understand why.
Cheer up my brother,
Live in the sunshine.
We'll understand it all by and by.

When peace was ruptured in our household, it was always because of Dad's quick and hot temper. There were quarrels about him being gone all the time, his pilfering the food money to buy booze and smoking tobacco. There was also the issue of his womanizing and not holding down a steady job. He often ended the argument by shouting and cursing, slamming the screen door, and leaving.

As time went on, Dad's rage became a major issue. He once borrowed a black man's wagon and team of mules. Clarence and I were with him at the time. One of the mules balked in the street and refused to move. Dad became enraged and rammed a pitchfork handle into the mule's rectum rupturing its intestines. The mule died, which caused a serious altercation between Dad and the mule's owner.

Dad had frequently beaten my oldest brother Charles from the time he was a small boy. Often, the beatings were severe. I am certain the issue was not that Charles refused to obey. But, like me, he probably didn't understand or respond quickly enough. Once, after Charles had angered him, Dad grabbed a hoe and threatened to kill him. Mama had to stand between him and my brother to prevent a disaster. Sometimes, she didn't know what inflamed his rage. She wrote about the incidents in her memoir:

"Martha was nearly three months old when Aubrey would have killed Charles if I hadn't of stepped in his way. Aubrey said he would have killed Charles if I hadn't been there."

On another occasion, when he threatened and cursed in his rage to beat Charles, Mama again stood between them and refused to budge. Dad went inside the house, yanked open the cabinet drawer, and pulled out a large knife. He turned toward Mama who was standing in the doorway. Mama thought that she, Charles, and Cathy were going to die. In uncontrollable fury, he stabbed the refrigerator door instead, sinking the knife to the hilt. Mama wrote about that incident as well:

"I froze in my tracks at the steps afraid he would chop me and little Cathy to pieces. Aubrey had missed a tiny space of killing Charles back in Dallas, in fact twice there three times he tried to kill me and three times little Charles; I said then for all concerned I had better get a divorce to protect the children and I from being killed and to protect Aubrey from killing one or two of us."

With that violent escalation of Dad's behavior, Mama called the police. Not long afterward, she filed for a divorce. Mama had long endured his indolence, lies, irresponsibility, selfishness, and unfulfilled promises. She had tolerated his misusing and abusing her. But Mama finally realized his uncontrollable rage made him a dangerous menace that she couldn't risk living with any longer.

The court granted Mama the divorce and ruled that Dad would have to stay away from our family. However, they gave him permission to come to the house one last time to get his belongings. I remember Dad gathering up his clothing, sheet music, and other items. He fumed and railed against Mama, the court system, and people in the town. Jay, the chief of police (the other policeman was a night cop and couldn't be there), was there to make certain he didn't hurt Mama.

In his memoir about that period, Dad wrote disingenuously, "I blame drudgery and mental distress as being responsible for my behavior."

When he was leaving, Dad cursed Mama and threatened to come back and kill her. At that point, Chief Jay grabbed him and tossed him into the police car. Dad was tall and muscled, but Chief Jay was built like a tank and feared no man.

Dad left Checotah that same day and went to California. I would not see him again for 23 years. He didn't say "goodbye" to any of his children before scampering away to begin his life afresh. Mama was burdened with six children, three boys and three girls, no money, and no job skills. After he left, he did not make any effort to pay child support or contact the children he was responsible for bringing into the world.

The first couple of months after Dad left were a bittersweet period. There was peace in the house, but we struggled to survive. We might have starved had it not been for Mama pleading for food from the few people she was acquainted with. The divorce was final September 3, 1953. Mama applied for Welfare assistance, but there was no indication of when the checks would begin arriving. Forty days later a compassionate postman who knew about the situation delivered Mama's first welfare check on Sunday evening, October 13th. She had reached the emotional bottom the Friday before, as she puts it, "so downhearted." Mama cashed the check on Monday. Her first purchase was groceries. That day, October 14, 1953, for the first time in our lives, we ate until we were full.

Mama realized that the welfare check would not be enough to feed us and pay the rent, so she began looking for a job. She had no car and, in fact, had still not learned how to drive. Her job opportunities were few. However, she found a job working in a slaughterhouse a quarter-mile across the pasture west of our house. The slaughterhouse processed animals the old fashioned way. Although she was a woman applying for a man's job, George, the owner, was kind enough to hire her.

Mama's small income, plus meat products from the slaughterhouse, and government welfare and commodities, helped feed her and six hungry mouths. Having been through the depression, she knew how to make use of every part of an animal. We often had beef byproducts mixed with eggs for breakfast. She worked very hard to feed her family.

Mama's mental and physical constitution was phenomenal. Not many men could have accomplished what she did. It was not a perfect life, but she managed to keep us children fed, clothed, and under a shelter. She could have run away and left the state with her burden. It must have been a temptation to shake off the harsh responsibility. She could have refused the daunting challenge of attempting that degree of motherhood with poverty as her constant antagonist. Most women might have done just that. But not Mama!

She planted a large garden in a plot of ground east of the house. I don't remember much about her working in the garden, but I do remember how she looked. Poignant in my memories is a colorful image of her in working garb. She didn't wear perfume or makeup. She always wore a dress, an apron, and a scarf or something on her head. There were stains under the arms of her man's shirt, and her clothing smelled like sweat. Her hair was tucked under a homemade cap, with her hands in cheap brown cotton gloves clutching a hoe handle. I can see her boots, an apron, and dirt-soiled hankie with which she wiped her sun-browned face.

She knew how precarious our situation was. There was no time to rest while the sun shined. There would be no one to help if grim circumstances rolled a dark cloud over our lives. We were not much help to her. Most of the time, I was more in her way than I was good at being a helper.

On washday, four lines of sheets, towels, shirts, dresses, and pants hung out to dry. The small washhouse stood between the house and garden. Often, I tried to help Mama sort clothes or run them through the wringer, a set of rubber rollers that squeezed out the water. Once, while putting wet clothes into the wringer, the rollers grabbed my fingers and began gobbling my arm. Terrified and standing on my tiptoes, I screamed for help. Before Mama could stop the old machine, the rollers had pulled me in past the elbow. That was the end of my working in the washhouse.

Mama raised a large flock of chickens that consisted mostly of white Leghorns with some Dominiques and Rhode Island Reds. Sometimes, we boys would chase down a chicken for supper. Chicken-catching wire in hand, we wove in and out of the sheets and under the clotheslines as the chicken ran for its life.

It was in the struggle to survive that we bonded. It was in the pressure the struggle produced that we separated. Had some things changed and others stayed the same, we might have flourished as a functional and emotionally healthy family. But Mama was not emotionally healthy. The pain of deep wounds and weariness of spirit wore on her.

As a virus, pain seeped its agony and qualm into every crack of our tenuous existence. It was easy for Mama to look around and see reasons for despair. Where would she go if we were forced to move? What if she became sick and couldn't work? Who would be there to help if sudden trouble dropped its anvil on us? So far away from family and so close to the edge, the pressure was immense.

Mama needed someone to say, "I love you." She needed appreciation and acknowledgment for her sacrifice. She needed a strong and confident husband to banish pain and its crushing doubt. But how could she hope for that? What man wants to marry a rugged woman with a six-child instant family?

Also feeding the mounting frustration was no doubt the portentous view of a sacrificial road extending years into a bleak future. There was the affliction of remorse that she had married an obstinately corrupt man. She had wasted her best years investing in a failure. Now she had half a dozen children to support while *he* was able to enjoy a fresh start; it was the searing reality of a life that was robbed and complicated by a Casanovian villain. Mama's main relief from the stress was to work. The other relief was the safety valve on the pressure cooker.

Eventually, the long and physically demanding hours in the slaughterhouse began to wear on Mama. She often came home from work so tired she could barely move. Additionally, she walked nearly a half-mile to and from work. Sometimes, the walk home would be in the dusk or dark. Often, she came home to a house ransacked by feral children. Many times, we failed to do our chores. We were as wild as unsupervised children could be.

I believe that because of Dad's abuse and rejection, the profusion of hurt stored in her heart was too traumatic for mothering so many children. At some point, the heaviness became too great to bear. She needed an outlet. We boys became the vent for the mounting pressure. No doubt, we could have worn the term rascals very well. As all unruly children, we pushed beyond the limits of tolerant behavior. Eventually, the lid blew on the pressure cooker. The dance was over—the fiddler had to be paid.

CHAPTER 3

MAMA'S WRATH

Violence again charged into our lives like an Oklahoma twister ripping through a thicket.

During that early period when we became too rowdy, or didn't obey her quickly enough, Mama sometimes erupted into a fit of rage. She whipped us with whatever she could get her hands on. In the beginning, she grabbed a switch from off the top of the refrigerator. Then she made us line up for our whippings. "Spare the rod, spoil the child," was her motto.

I wasn't the only one who was beaten, though, to my knowledge, Mama never whipped the girls. Once, when my brother was whipped first, I watched him being flogged with the switch, dancing about and crying with unchecked emotion, and stark terror filled my heart. His cries and Mama's admonitions incited an inferno of reality that the same thing was going to happen to me, and there was no way to avoid it.

Then it was my turn. When Mama grabbed my arm, I was frozen with fear. As the lashing began, I became delirious with fear and pain. I had never experienced anything that traumatic up to that point in my young life. My life consisted of being secure in my own foggy little world, so I came out of it like a bear cub exiting the den right into the face of a raging forest fire.

I have no doubt that Mama's decision to use the switch was partly because of an ancestral paradigm. My Grandma Barnes was a disciplinarian. It was not uncommon in those days to have visits to the woodshed and being flogged with a switch, belt, or homemade paddle. However, when corporal punishment began in our house, it had a devastating effect on me. It was like I had entered a nightmare. Everything changed, and nothing would ever change it back.

Today, I am incapable of measuring or adequately explaining the effects of that experience on my young psyche. I look back on it as viewing someone else's life. The only way I can describe it is succinct, probably insufficient, and perhaps inadequate. Life exploded, and some of the pieces were lost.

Mama's whippings were in perfect cadence with her reprimands—each word accompanied by a strike of the switch. "I-told-you-to-straighten-up-this-house!" Or, "When-I-say-do-something-you'd-better-listen!" She sometimes added, "You-hear-me?" It was like Rap with a slap. Each boy was whipped with a variation of the admonition. We lived in cautious fear for a long period after one of those episodes.

The switches on top of the refrigerator were eventually replaced. They often broke in two or came apart with her fury. Unsatisfied, she fashioned a discipline device. She whittled a stout rod out of a hickory limb. Around the top of the rod, she carved a groove and tied a narrow belt with a shoelace. The belt was cut in two pieces and the tips tapered to points. She then split the pointed ends of the two pieces and augered holes in them. The short whip transferred her wrath adequately. No matter how much force she applied, it never came apart.

One of her frequent sayings was, "I'll whip you till the blood runs down your heels!" Another one she would say when she was coming after me with a switch or the whip was, "I'll give you something you'll live to tell your grandkids about!" Hearing her feet angrily stomping on the heart-pine floor as she headed toward the kitchen filled me with terror. I never knew if I was the target or if it was one of my brothers.

During the beatings, I cried passionately and uncontrollably. I begged her to stop, but to no avail. After one beating, I sobbed deeply. It was more than the pain of the beating on my body—it was a thick, dark hurt oozing from the brokenness inside my heart. It was the reality that my small world wasn't safe—that the same person I depended on for food and a home could be my worst nightmare if I provoked her.

My crying irritated her. Mama issued another one of her common threats, "You stop that crying, or I will give you something to cry about."

Sometimes, I simply could not stop. She jerked me up by the arm and lashed me several more times. The whip wrapped around my body, striking the soft tissue beneath my arms. The holes and slits in the straps bruised the flesh and left red welts that became swollen.

I pled and promised to quit crying if she would stop. When she let me go, I ran into the bedroom I shared with my brothers. Although I feared the dark, at that moment, I did not believe anything in the dark could be worse than what I had experienced in the light. My pain obliterated my fear. Sometimes I crouched in a corner whimpering. The deep pain wanted to erupt. It felt as if I would die if I kept it down. I went into the closet where we tossed our dirty clothes and buried my face in the pile of clothing. Then my small frame convulsed with the raw emotional lava. I still feared she would hear me, so I choked off the eruption several times to listen for her footsteps.

One time, I heard her call my full name. I knew what that meant and instinctively ran out the door. My mind was filled with fright. The first command that came to my mind was "run!" And run I did. I dashed for the old barn as fast as my little legs could pump, hoping to hide in a cubbyhole in the crumbling structure. I was too terrified to look back and see how close she was. Every muscle was electrified. My brain was on fire with fear and adrenalin. I could hear her screaming. Her words vibrating with anger pierced the fog of terror in my mind. "Don't you run away from me! You wait'll I catch you. I'll whip you till the blood runs down your heels!"

I had done something wrong, but I didn't know what it was. All I knew for certain was that if she caught me, I would become overwhelmed with pain. I trembled to think of the sharp sting of the switch as it struck and then raked across my flesh leaving fine bloody lines through the welts. It wasn't just the pain, but the anger and brute force dominance that reduced me to helplessness and hopelessness. No one was going to help me. I would be at the mercy of a violent adult bigger than me and with no inclination for mercy.

So I fled for safety in the only hiding place on the property. However, when I reached the barn I opted to race beyond it, crawled under the barbed wire fence, and disappeared into the tall weeds. Crouched in my hiding place, I watched as Mom stopped at the fence. She scanned the weeds for what seemed like a long period. I was certain she could hear my breathing and heart pounding.

"You have to come home sooner or later. You're going to have to take your medicine." With that, she left. I crawled to the edge of the weeds and watched her go into the house.

Later in the day, the sun hung low in the west and darkness began to fall. I knew I couldn't stay outside all night. With my fear of the dark, there was no place to go but home. *Maybe she'll not be as mad*, I thought. *Maybe it won't be a bad whipping.*

I decided to go inside and take my punishment. I was tired, emotionally drained, thirsty, and very hungry. I was also subdued and lonely. I wanted to be with my family and for everything to be normal again. But I wasn't normal and would never be so. The world I lived in wasn't normal. It was the small world of a dysfunctional family that had never known anything other than deep poverty, instability, and distress. Because it was the only world I knew, I was ready to suffer to be in it again.

Mama whipped me that night as I expected, but halfheartedly on the buttocks and without her usual proclamations. I still wept from pain but also deep dejection. It wasn't just about the beatings. In fact, I eventually believed and accepted that all children were beaten by their parents. And perhaps many of them were.

I wept bitterly because I didn't understand her rage. When Mama went off on a rant declaring I had sassed her, or didn't obey, I could not remember having done it. She never told me why I was wrong—only that I was wrong. When it was made brutally clear to me that I was wrong, I believed it solely on the basis of my punishment. I had no hope to believe there was any way my situation would change.

Even though I was just a kid, my young mind tried to process the injustice. I just could not do it. The punishment did not fit the crime. I wondered, *was I really that bad?* It felt like complete rejection. I went through that period insecure and somewhat shell shocked. To this day, I have the feeling I'm the one who is wrong when people disagree with me. Although I may know beyond any doubt I am not in error, I continue to feel condemnation.

Six years old

I came to fear and hate the hickory whip. I do not remember how many times Mama beat me. It was not every day or every week. However, the reality and dread that I was in constant danger of her wrath was embedded in my small mind. Although I have forgotten the number, I will never forget the worst beatings. However, because of God's love, I have forgiven her, and I am healed.

My oldest brother Charles took the brunt of the beatings. He had already suffered mentally from Dad's beatings. Mama's whippings and the bullying at school added to his brokenness. One day, Mama whipped him violently. While she was beating him, he broke through a window to escape. He suffered several cuts on his hands and in other places. Chief Jay came and talked to Mama. After that, the beatings were rare. Tragically, the end to the violence came too late for Charles. He was twice placed in the state mental health facility. In my opinion, he remains affected by the damage of that abuse.

To be fair, I have to consider Mama's side of the story. In retrospect, I have a better understanding of why she angrily exploded under the pressure. From reading her memoir and realizing all she went through, it is obvious she was also hurt, abused, and frustrated.

Sometimes, I visited the slaughterhouse where Mama worked. I have a vivid memory of her standing, waiting for an animal to be killed so it could be processed. She waited stoically with her tan stockings rolled halfway between her knees and ankles. Her hair was tucked under a homemade cap that more resembled a blousy beret. Hands stuffed in long rubber gloves hung at her side. Clutched in her right hand was a long, tapered knife covered with blood. Her face and clothing were splattered with blood, and the floor was stained the color of it. There she stood in her rubber boots on a partially washed section of that floor.

As I think about that image today, my heart is filled with admiration mixed with sadness and love for her. When one adds up the rejection and abuse by my Dad, being burdened with six children to shelter, clothe, and feed, and carrying a dead dream in her soul, I wonder how she did it. How did she feel having to work as a man? What did it do to her sense of dignity and femininity?

Did she ever become discouraged or depressed when she looked back over her life? What were her dreams and goals? Yes, she was a harsh disciplinarian, but I wonder if she was just pushed to the breaking point from everything combined. Back then, there was no way I could have realized or understood the effect all those factors had on her.

Further, there was no way she could have known what the whippings were doing to me and my brothers. She was no doubt acting out the discipline she had experienced and witnessed growing up in Warren. She wasn't a monster. The combination of factors had a root of pain to attach to. Her behavior was the amalgamation of emotional damage and pressure.

Mama—full of pain and rage

Mama was not simply an ignorant hick. She was also an accomplished seamstress. She made most of our clothing, especially shirts for the boys and dresses for the girls. Somewhere, I have pictures of a cowboy shirt she made for me to wear on the day school pictures were taken. I still have a quilt she made.

She had many talents that she put on hold to raise her family. After all the kids were gone, Mama started needle pointing again. The first item she finished was a bedspread she had started twenty years earlier. One of her friends talked her into entering it into the State Fair. She won first place!

There would be many more artful items that would come from those thick, callused, and arthritic fingers. She was a woman who could work like a man, build houses, smoke houses, barns, saw and chop wood, and every other skill involving hard labor. And yet she made a prize-winning needlepoint bedspread and beautiful dresses.

Maybe she didn't look like a lady. Some of my classmates made sport of her and called her names. She didn't have great social skills. She wasn't "movie star" pretty. Few men came asking for a date. Her life work was being a Mama, "dad," and breadwinner to six children. Yes, she beat me. But, in her own way, she must also have loved me. How could I have broken her heart so badly if she had not loved me? Why didn't she leave us and start a new life somewhere far away if it wasn't love that compelled her to stay? I love and respect her today for the amazing woman she was.

CHAPTER 4

KING OF TRASH

There were some good times when I managed to somewhat stay under the radar and out of Mama's way. We had very few store-bought toys to play with. Our playthings were stick horses and rifles and toys rescued from the city dump, which was a cornucopia of toys and other interesting items. It was located about a quarter mile through the pasture. The garbage became irresistible and drew us like a magnet. Foraging in the dump became one of the favorite activities of my brothers and me.

Amazingly, we made the trips there and back and did all the foraging in our bare feet. We never wore shoes during the entire summer. I can remember the sensitive process of toughening my feet after shedding my winter brogans. It didn't take long before we were able to walk on the hot dirt without pain. However, what had become our toy supply and favorite occupation also became our social albatross.

On my first day of school, I discovered what people thought about foragers in the dump. Until that day, I had no inkling of a social standard by which people were judged. I knew Charles didn't like school. He had told us about being bullied. Some of the boys ganged up and tormented him with catcalls and mocking. Charles was big for his age and naturally muscled up, but he did not want to fight. He often carried his Bible to school. The reason for the torment became clear on that fateful first morning.

I rose early that morning as usual. I was so excited that I had trouble sleeping the night before. Getting to attend school was to me both an adventure and a coming of age. No matter what my older brothers had told me about school, I was eager to see and experience it myself.

Breakfast was always scrambled eggs, gravy, biscuits, and a glass of milk. Then it was out the door into the moderate chill of the autumn morning. The orangey sun had begun to spray its ethereal light across the pasture. The dawn was so low on the flat Oklahoma horizon that the fence posts cast long shadows into the neighbor's foggy pasture. On a bright day, there wasn't anything much higher than a pond bank as far as the eye could see.

The three of us tromped through the dewy grass, kicking milkweeds and otherwise meandering toward the designated bus stop. The anticipation of riding the school bus was exciting but also a bit dreadful. But traveling through the pasture with my brothers that first morning made me feel important—and older.

As we waited on that cool, dew-drenched morning, I could not resist walking the few steps into the dump to dig about. I heard the bus coming, but I wasn't in any great hurry to get out of the dump before it arrived. In fact, it never occurred to me that I was doing anything inappropriate. I foolishly thought I was lucky to live so near such a great place.

Even before the folding doors of the bus opened, I heard the commotion from the kids. They had pulled down the bus windows and were jeering. Their taunts and derision dripped with contempt. When I got on the bus, they began singing a song they had made up about my brothers. This time, I felt their scorn. It was something like:

> *Once there were three Fisher boys,*
> *Once there were three Fisher boys,*
> *They love to play inside the trash,*
> *Their Mama wears a big mustache,*
> *Once there were three Fisher boys*

At first, I was stunned. I had never been ridiculed before. When I realized we were being derided, it was like a cold slap in the face. I was enraged but could do nothing about it. Humiliated, red-faced, and angry, I sat at the back of the bus with my head down. We were labeled as the "dump kids." Eventually, they called us "white trash."

The way to begin building peer acceptance was not waiting for the bus at the entrance of the city dump. I had committed social suicide on the first day of school and didn't know it. Mama didn't understand what it was doing to us. Besides, with her going to work early in the morning, there was no other suitable way to get to school at that time.

At first, I retaliated when kids bullied me at school. I would curse and fight them. I could not understand why they were rude. It felt like they were punishing me for not doing or being something, but I didn't know what it was. If their purpose was to make me feel inferior and worthless, I already had all of that I could stand. Initially, I refused to accept that they were better than me. I stubbornly rejected that there was anything wrong with foraging in the dump.

After school, when the bus pulled up in front of the city dump to let us off, the derision began again. We didn't have to put up with it long because we got off the bus and quickly started toward home. But that was merely a pretense. When we reached the ditch on the side of the road, we hugged the dirt bank near the pasture fence. After the bus was completely out of sight, we raced to the dump to stake claims on our piles of trash.

After some time, I realized they had branded me for life. School was like entering another world. At home, I was part of the family. At school, I was a social reject, someone who deserved complete and unwavering disrespect. Of course, at the time, my young mind could never grasp that logic. However, I felt their contemptuous words and actions eating into the depth of my being. Had I known that I had a soul, I might have wept for what they were doing to it.

One day, I watched some guys surround my oldest brother and begin to torment him. They were large enough to cause some damage, but he was larger. It was very sad to watch. I wanted to help him, but I was too small. He pulled a pair of scissors from under his shirt and threatened to kill them.

A teacher arrived and made them all leave. Shortly after, Chief Jay showed up and gave Charles a ride home. I was enraged at what they had done to him. I purposed that I would never allow them to do such a thing to me no matter what I had to do to stop them.

Eventually, I realized the die was cast. I would always be a target, and there did not appear to be any way to change that fact. Just as I had done at home, I tried to avoid their scorn by staying under the radar. Added to their list of reasons to reject me was the fact they viewed me as different.

After several years of school, I gradually realized what I had not previously recognized about myself. I came to the reality that I was different and not in a good way. It was as if I had been born defective—that something was missing. At home with my siblings,

I had never had that feeling. However, the distinction was made painfully clear by the bullying. They knew I was different and being different was all it took to become a target.

To say I was socially awkward might be an understatement. Either I was very quiet, or I would blurt out something everyone would scoff or derisively laugh at. However, it was something more than social awkwardness. It was like everyone knew what to do but me. They knew the nuances of social interaction. I didn't even know the rules of the game.

It felt like punishment, but I didn't know the reason I was being punished. Their bullying became an extension of the trauma of Mama's beatings in its effect on my mind and spirit.

Not all or even most of my classmates bullied me. On occasion, older kids joined in the sport. A few of my kinder classmates tried to console me. But I was inconsolable. The fact is, I did not know how to accept kindness. Their overtures made me nervous, and I closed up like a clam.

Sometimes I wondered what there was about me personally that caused the bullying. I wondered if I was ugly. Sometimes

7 years old

I looked in the mirror and believed the person looking back was ugly. I also thought, *maybe I'm doing something wrong. I do not remember doing anything to irritate anyone.* But then, we always remember the foibles of others while conveniently forgetting our own.

Nevertheless, I never understood how to interact with other kids. It continued throughout my childhood and adolescence. I never accepted the bullying and place in the pecking order assigned to me. I began to hate the ones who had assigned it to me. It wasn't until I approached adolescence that I totally rejected the pecking order. I became determined that I would not live in their social basement.

Eventually, their torment got through to me. Their sneering derision had been like a mirror held before me, and I now saw what they saw in me. They identified me as a freak, and I realized it was true. With that reality, I became terrified when any attention was focused on me.

It became my goal to reach the end of the day and go home to my sanctuary. Although there was a possibility I could be whipped there, it was home. I could be alone. No one taunted and ridiculed me. Home was a different world. It was the world I knew before school took away my real self. It was the place where I last had it.

Their taunts may have bent me, but I was not broken. The dump became my therapy—and my castle. They didn't ever have to know about it. I may have been king of the bottom to them, but in the city dump, at least I knew who I was. I was Cedric, not the bullied one, but the smudged and triumphant one—king of trash.

CHAPTER 5

RESTLESS

Like every other kid, I was ecstatic and relieved each year when school ended. When the bell rang for that last time, I was like a young horse in a fresh pasture. Spring soon gave way to summer, which became a season of purging and growing. Summer's experiences washed out the stain of social scorn. The joy of freedom faded their mockery like yesterday's shadows. I repressed the memories of rejection and reveled in the wonderful sense of reckless independence. It was as if school never happened. The social shame no longer invaded my private and uninterrupted world. Over the summer, I regained my identity, such as it was.

However, the euphoria of being released from the regime of school soon subsided. I initially settled into life in our small world with its limited experiences. Other than hearing about a house fire or someone dying, there were few spikes of excitement. We were isolated from everything happening elsewhere in society. As most poor families, we still didn't have a television.

Once, we were invited to visit the neighbors across the pasture whose house was a few hundred yards east of the city dump. They had just bought a television. It was a fascinating experience, but they did not invite us again. Our large family crowding their living room made it an awkward situation. It would be years before I watched television again. The radio became our connection to the rest of the world.

When we got our first radio, it was an old used one and rather large. It was brown with a speaker built into the front of its arched face. Someone strung the wire antenna on several posts planted a good distance across the yard and out into the pasture. We would gather around it in the evenings to listen to "The Shadow," "The Lone Ranger," "Amos and Andy," and other shows.

Then there was the music.

The music, especially the live programs, was enthralling. I don't believe we missed a Saturday night of the Grand Ole Opry for many years. I didn't even know what the instruments were that made all those sounds, especially the crazy sound of Cousin Jody's lap steel. But the music reverberated in my soul.

One day, we went to a jamboree being held downtown in the local theater. The band included a banjo player, upright bass player, a couple of fiddle and guitar players, and a mandolin player. It was the first time I actually saw individuals playing instruments other than a piano or organ. I knew immediately I wanted to play guitar.

Dad had never bothered to teach us anything about music. We did not have any musical instruments in the house, so I made my own. It was a crude thing, a short piece of board with steeples on one end and a few bailing wires strung down the middle. I "tuned" the "strings" by wrapping them around screws on the other end and then tightening them. By sliding the metal handle of a case knife along the "strings" and picking the other end with whatever stiff plastic I could find, I made melodies. The instrument would change tuning overnight, so I had to re-tune or learn how to play it again the next day.

I learned to sing listening to the radio. Perhaps my musical talent was inherited from Dad. However, when she was young, Mama had played the guitar and sang. Several of her brothers had been professional musicians. Thus, it is likely that my love and ability to sing came also from her side of the family.

Once, when I was probably around nine years old, a couple of black kids came over. I stood on a chest in the house and sang to them and my brothers and sisters. I sang songs I had heard on the radio. One song was "Pistol-Packing Mama":

Lay that pistol down, Babe.
Lay that pistol down.
Pistol packin' mama
Lay that pistol down.

Another one was "My Baby Loves the Western Movies":

Ah . . . um . . . my baby loves the Western movies.
My baby loves the Western movies,
Bam, bam, shoot 'em up Pow.
Ah . . . um . . . My babe loves the Western Movies.

When it came to the "bam, bam, shoot 'em up, pow," I tried to make the sounds of a pistol as I heard them on the radio.

On another occasion, I stood on the edge of the porch and preached. My siblings sat on the grass or stood while I preached to them. I didn't have much to say, but I mimicked as best I could the preacher in the church we attended. I was wearing hand-me-down bibbed overalls without a shirt. As I preached, I waved my hands and pointed as I had seen the pastor do.

Most of the time, I was left alone. I would lie on the dry grass and gaze up at the clouds and wonder about the sky and life. I marveled at the clouds, the occasional plane that soared overhead, and tried to make some sense of things. Nothing really made sense to me except whatever intrusion forced me to acknowledge it. Those intrusions included surviving school and trying not to get in trouble with Mama. Beyond that, I had no purpose, and my identity only existed in my imaginative world. I don't know how to explain it, but there seemed to be something missing that I could not identify. It was a missing piece of a puzzle, but I didn't know what to search for.

Consequently, I always felt alone, like I was out of place and couldn't understand how to fit in. Maybe it was the same way many other young people felt. But the feeling of being a misfit always brought with it the feeling of inferiority. When the pressure of living in a world I didn't understand became too great, I defaulted to my private world filled with daydreams and wild imaginations.

During that particular summer of my ninth year, something began to manifest in my nature I can only identify as restlessness. Maybe it had always been there, but I had not recognized it before. At times, it was overpowering. It made sitting still in church or school difficult. When I was not reading a book, I always had to be doing something. The restlessness continually drove me. My attention span was short, and I was constantly looking for something interesting.

The restlessness compelled me to expand the boundaries and explore the world around me. Heading into the neighborhood was out of the question. The phobia of going beyond our gate and into "colored town" was too ingrained. I could not vanquish the sense of being an intruder twenty feet the other side of the gate. Perhaps as a white boy in a black community, I was intruding. If so, it was the consequence of suspicion and unreasonable societal rules that beget division. I had not heard of or experienced racism at that point in my life.

However, I was changing and becoming bored with our gated compound which became smaller as I grew. I became unable to focus on anything for very long. Further, I developed an insatiable penchant for learning and discovering new things and experiences. So I visited the slaughterhouse where Mama worked. It was fascinating to watch the entire process of butchering, but I could not bear it when they processed sheep. Their pitiful and terrified bleating cut to the core of my spirit.

Thus, I returned to the only thing I knew of that was always changing and providing something new. I headed through the north pasture to the city dump. I spent much of the summer searching through trash for discarded items, broken radios, and other gadgets. Distracted by her long workdays, Mama didn't seem to care if I was absent all day every day. That left me with many days of unsupervised freedom. Mama's one requirement was that I would come home before supper time.

At some point, I decided to go deeper into the dump. I saw vehicles head into the maze of dirt roads and wanted to investigate what they had dumped. When I was younger, I went so far into that place, I almost got lost. It wasn't that the dump was that large but that I was so small. Now older, I headed deeper into the dump and discovered a veritable treasure-trove of bicycle frames, wheels, and some parts.

I brought home the conglomeration of parts and began assembling them into a working bike. Eventually, I managed to put one together, but I didn't have the money to purchase tubes and tires. So I learned how to ride by peddling the bike on its rims in the soft dirt road of our driveway. But eventually that also became boring. I wanted to experience something else more challenging. I was seeking adventure but didn't know where to find it. It was a restless quest to spice my dull and monotonous life with excitement.

My restlessness became worse as the start of school approached. I felt that the summer had flown by uneventfully. So one day I made a fishing pole out of a willow limb, dug up some worms, and went fishing for the first time in the pond at the end of the pasture. Finally, I had something exciting to do. It was thrilling to watch the cork sink, yank on the line, and pull out a fish. I wanted to go fishing every day. However, later in the summer, I became afraid of the water. That fear developed because of a vivid incident that occurred one very hot summer day.

I heard a siren and saw the red lights of an ambulance. There was a commotion near the middle of the field on the south side of our house. The field was parallel to the backside of "colored town." I raced up the fencerow to where a crowd of black adults and children had gathered. I arrived just in time to see them pull a young black boy face down from a small pond. He was not moving. He never responded to their efforts to revive him.

It was a terrifying and poignant scene that followed. The paramedics placed his body on a stretcher and covered his face with a sheet. A woman, perhaps his mother, began wailing with such a deep passion and sorrow that it stirred angst and dread deep in my spirit. Others started crying. The young boys stood with shock as they watched their friend, and possibly a brother, being taken away.

I realized in that moment that water could kill me. However, I also realized I could die at any age. And where would I go? At church, the preacher talked about Hell and of how the wicked will go to Hell. He explained that good people go to Heaven. I wondered if I would go to Heaven when I died. I did not believe I was good because Mama and my classmates had made it brutally clear that I was not. But I did not know if I was wicked. Until I knew if I were wicked, I purposed to stay away from the pond we passed on the way to the dump. As for being good, I hoped that one day I would find a way to accomplish that.

CHAPTER 6

WALL OF HATE

When summer vacation came to an end, anxiety seeped into my mind. Summer winding down to the start of school was like watching a bad ending to a good story. The only thing I liked about school was the library. However, I would gladly have lost that privilege if I did not have to attend school. I would have begged Mama to let me quit school, but there was no possibility she would agree to that.

The arrival of the first day was my cue to settle again into my role as the unnoticeable one, which wasn't that hard to do. Every weekday, I got up in the morning and mechanically went through the routine. Everything about going to school was drudgery. I didn't like waiting for the bus at the city dump and certainly did not like riding it. Nothing about school made me want to go. I endured it because there was no option.

From the first morning bus ride, the kids riding the bus picked up where they left off the previous year. The cacophony of jeers and crude remarks were the same. I continued to be the occasional butt of scornful remarks and practical jokes on the playground. However, the new grade level came with different teachers, and a couple of the teachers appeared to despise me. One of them was Mrs. Mackie, a red-headed and very condescending woman who picked on me regularly. She paddled me not long into the school season for a minor offense.

Once, my classmates told her I had said something bad to them in the schoolyard during recess. I was guilty. I remember so clearly what I said. I told one kid who was pushing me around, "You take a booger from your nose and eat it!" They excitedly ran to tell the teacher what I had said. Then they sat on the edge of their seats to see what she would do to me. When Mrs. Mackie disciplined me with the paddle, I was more than angry. I felt something powerful rise up from the depths. It was rage and hatred.

Another time, she called me up to the front of the class as an example of poor personal hygiene. She forced me to turn my back on the class as she grabbed my ears and pulled them, revealing the dirt. Then she would explain why they should all wash regularly. I had hated her for paddling me. But after her lesson in hygiene, my hatred consumed me.

I hated her bland face. I hated her monotone voice. I hated her red hair. I hated her glasses. I hated her plump body. And I hated her slight condescending smile and soulless eyes as she ridiculed me in front of the class. My imagination ran wild as malice and vengeance seethed in my mind. I imagined pummeling her with my fists until I was spent of the last drop of energy.

Mrs. Mackie was correct about my hygiene. We took baths every Saturday night and never during the week. No doubt my brothers and I were dirty and had unkempt appearances. But we did not realize anything was different about us. Mama never said anything about washing behind our ears. We often wore the same clothes for days. Mine were handed down from my brothers. Mama always bought us brogans to wear because they lasted much longer than shoes. So we must have appeared as Oklahoma hillbillies.

However, that harsh exposure of me as a bad example fueled and grew a resident resentment and anger that remained just under the surface. As rejection by classmates at school became more pronounced, I came to the realization that I had to hide in broad daylight to avoid it. I stayed away from many of the activities. As a chameleon, I blended with the background and kept quiet. These experiences together became the formative qualities of my hatred and mistrust of society in general.

I tried to bury with hatred the strong and constant aware-ness of inferiority. Maybe I wasn't born with inferiority, but it felt like it had always been there. I fought the painful sense of nothingness with everything I had, but it never went away. I eventually accepted that something about me personally offended and repulsed people. The flawed and pain-manipulated thought process which led me to that conclusion was never challenged. There was no sense of achievement, no honors or accolades, and no commendations. I began to believe everyone despised me. Most likely, the majority probably seldom noticed me and never thought about me.

My desire to achieve, to be accepted and normal, created a war with the inferiority. I wanted out of the torment. There were times that suicide would have been an option had I not been so afraid to die. I heard preachers say so much about Hell that I didn't want to go there. And I was certain I would be cast into Hell if I died.

I was finally old enough to begin walking to school, thus avoiding harassment on the bus ride. I once tried walking through "colored town" but I had an encounter with a couple of black kids who tried to beat me up. I avoided that altercation by outrunning them. So I walked through the field west of our house and past the slaughterhouse where Mama worked. Then I could get on the railroad tracks and walk all the way into town without anyone bothering me. I still had to be wary of the dogs that sometimes ran in packs. However, it was worth the risk to avoid enduring the daily torment on the bus.

Along with hating to go to school, I became very reluctant to attend church meetings.

We always went to church every Sunday morning. I didn't totally understand most of what went on there. The first church we attended did not allow musical instruments. The second had a piano and organ. The music was better, but I didn't enjoy singing the hymns, which I did not understand. However, every Sunday morning, Mama woke up her large brood, made us put on our finest clothes, and down the road we went.

It must have been a sight—Mama walking along carrying or holding hands with the youngest with five siblings plugging along behind. In church, we heard about Hell and damnation, and the need to "get saved." Charles "got saved," but the rest of us were too young. However, before my salvation could occur in that church, Mama had a falling-out with the pastor.

I won't say much about the reason for that conflict except to say Mama met an older man, Charlie, who showed her kindness and respect. He lived with us for a few years before he died. At the time he died, Mama was in a hospital in one town having major surgery while he was in one in another town. He died of stomach cancer when she was still in the hospital. During that time, a wonderful and godly old black woman who lived a couple of houses down the street took care of us. She had become one of Mama's dearest friends. When she died, Mama and us kids walked a couple of miles to her church for the funeral. We were the only white people there.

After Mama's clash with the pastor, we began attending a much larger church on the other side of town. That meant more walking for the family, but we sometimes got a ride. I didn't like it there.

In my mind, it was a city church and full of citified people. Some of my classmates, who often tormented me in school, went to that church. When I was forced to sit beside some of them, they would go to another pew or move away from me.

There were two humiliating incidents that happened to me in that church. The first one spiked such a rage in me that had I been older or had a weapon, I would probably have seriously injured or killed the offender.

One older boy enjoyed tormenting me. I had witnessed him bullying other young boys, so I tried to stay clear of him. Although I was not a weakling, I was very scrawny. The larger boy often pushed me around and sometimes became rough. Every time he attended church, I tried to be as inconspicuous as possible.

However, on one Sunday night everyone was playing tag or some other game that involved running and contact outside. I tried to join in the fun and forgot about the guy. Seemingly out of nowhere, he tackled me. I was no match for his strength. He immediately pinned me to the ground. Then he sat on my face and flatulated.

He got up and ran off laughing as everyone who witnessed his deed laughed. No doubt, I had inherited my Dad's raging temper. All I could think of was killing him. Of all the memories of church, that is the one that to this day humiliated me the most. It was as if I had been discarded as toilet waste. I could not conceive of a more thorough and conclusive destruction of what remained of my self-esteem.

There were other incidents of humiliation but none that have with them the helplessness of being overpowered and treated as trash by someone for the sole reason that they could do it. I felt myself slipping down into darkness. The strong urge for fight or flight manifested. If I had surrendered to flight, I think I would have eventually committed suicide. However, I chose to fight. I refused to accept their insults and consigning me to worthlessness.

I kept telling myself that one day I would become famous and rich. I would force them to see how wrong they were. I began to despise Christians and church about that time.

It was wrong to judge the entire church and all Christians by that boy's actions. The guy was most likely not even a Christian. He probably came to church out of small-town boredom—simply to have some excitement and fun. But I never considered any of that logic. I had to fight against something in me that threatened to overwhelm my self-control. It was shame, and deep, dark, pain of rejection that burned in my brain so fiercely that I had no other thoughts but violence.

I still did not understand people, how to fit in, and could not reason why people behaved the way they did. It was as if they were from a better world filled with clever and confident people, and I was from an inferior one filled with rejects. From that perspective, it felt like injustice—as if I were being assigned perpetual punishment for which I had committed no other crime than to exist.

The second incident caused me to completely reject Christianity. It is the event when I "got saved." I don't remember my age or Clarence's age when we "got saved" and joined the church. In spite of Mama's discipline, we were still as ornery as two mostly unsupervised boys might be.

When Mama was at work, Clarence and I used to curse. We would say every vulgarity that we had heard from other kids and adults. In those days, men were respectful of their language around women and in a public place but not when they worked or conversed with other men. So we picked up their language. Although we knew it was wrong because Mama said so, we didn't know how wrong it was. We cursed stray dogs, cursed the heat, cursed people we didn't like (and they were a few choice ones) and cursed just to be cursing.

We never cursed Mama, but we cursed our Sunday School teacher. She was one of Mama's good friends, a lawyer's wife, and I believe she probably helped us financially on several occasions. Mrs.

Emma was hard on us in the Sunday School class. If we fidgeted or didn't pay attention, she would admonish us. Clarence and I appeared to be the only ones she corrected. I believe she was doing it because we were poor white trash. We resented her constant admonishing in front of the class.

One day, we drew unflattering pictures of her and wrote captions using some of our vulgarity. The next Sunday after church, and when people were still milling about inside, we rolled the paper up and put it in the door handle of her car. We were so covert that we thought no one would catch us. But we didn't fool anyone. Later that evening, Mama called us in the front room and informed us she knew we were the guilty ones. I believed at that point I was in for the worst beating ever. However, she and Mrs. Emma had struck a deal. All would be forgiven if we apologized to Mrs. Emma, walked down to the front of the church, repented, and "got saved."

I'm certain now that Mrs. Emma had good intentions. I do not believe that vengeance was in her mind when she came up with her plan. She likely wanted me to go to Heaven.

My resentment toward Mrs. Emma and Mama turned into something else that morning. I cannot explain what being forced to "get saved" did to me. I had heard many altar calls. I knew about salvation and had felt strongly compelled to go to the altar several times. However, it was clear to me that it was supposed to be a choice. But I had no real choice in the matter of my soul and the decision to become a Christian. I either had to do it or get beaten. I felt violated in the most sacred part of my core.

I believe that was the point when the hatred that ebbed and flowed from deep within began to be part of my conscious nature. I hated Mrs. Emma, I hated everyone involved, I hated Mama, I hated everything about the church, I hated everyone at school, and I hated everyone in Checotah. It was as if something had been desecrated that should not have been meddled with. Something sacred had been reduced to worthlessness.

After the humiliation by the older boy, I felt I didn't have anything left but my indefatigable independence. It was my soul. Earlier in my childhood, I did not know I had a soul. However, over the years of attending church, the preachers I listened to had often referred to man's eternal soul. It was what we were often entreated to give to God. Too many people had taken parts of my soul away from me. I felt I had nothing left to give.

Some reading my story may wonder why I didn't just get over those incidents. Why didn't I stop being a "big baby" and man up? Everyone goes through hardships and harsh experiences. They may wonder why I couldn't just say, "That's life" and rise above the fray. Why did I let those experiences go deep and simmer in me?

The answer is that I had no control over how they affected me. Whereas some people may have a mental or emotional defense system that stops pain at the door of their soul, or they have the ability to quickly eject it, I had no such barrier or ability. I was like a boy with no skin. The nerves were bare and unprotected. The germs could infect at will.

When I was treated cruelly or someone said something very degrading, my soul was like a sponge. Their humiliation would instantly flood my mind and emotional system. It felt like my brain and soul were on fire. I couldn't think clearly. My entire body tingled with shame and rage. I either slunk off in total defeat or retaliated. The truth is, I was somehow emotionally deformed. I did not know what to do but build a wall of hate and hide behind it.

Subsequently, every experience, both good and bad, was greatly magnified and prolonged in my mind. Memories of the discipline from Mama, the experience with Mrs. Emma, and the bad treatment at school overwhelmed me; it was to such an extent that I was completely incapable of feeling or thinking about anything else. My mind was in cloudiness so thick that I could not bear to be noticed. I became very quiet and withdrawn during those periods.

Furthermore, and the worst part was, I stored the pain and shame like a pile of nuclear waste. Years later, I would remember an event and rage would immediately rise up in my mind. Thoughts of vengeance would be right on its heels. I was a ticking time bomb who wanted to make people pay for my pain. Had I not invested myself in music, I do not know how I would have survived.

Charlie and Mama

CHAPTER 7

A MOVE TO THE COUNTRY

When I was about eleven years old, a circus came to town and set up in the field behind our house. People had to come through our yard to get to the circus. One was an old man who came to the house and asked Mama for a drink of water. They ended up sitting on the porch sipping water and talking. He returned several times to sit in the cool of the evenings and chat with Mama. They became good friends. That friendship would last until he died.

Mr. Willis was all we ever called him. His head was as bald as a cue ball, and his mouth often had dark crusty edges at the corners. He was a tobacco chewer and prolific spitter. When he talked, it was a slow drawl, as if he thought over virtually every word. Most of his paragraphs were punctuated by spitting a stream of tobacco juice at whatever target he chose. Sometimes it would be a fly or a bug whose misfortune it was to light or crawl within range.

Sometime after Mama became acquainted with Mr. Willis, our landlady asked Mama to move out so her old bachelor brothers would have a place to live. When he learned about the eviction notice, Mr. Willis offered us a place to live in the country. The old country house we moved into was completely void of paint. Mama and the girls had their own bedrooms, and we boys slept on pallets in the living room. The kitchen, living, and dining areas were all one room. Mama had to cook on an old wood cook stove as she had many years ago in Dallas. There was no indoor plumbing, so we drew water from a well. Fifty yards from the house was an outhouse toilet.

We boys took turns stoking the old potbellied wood stove early in the morning. Another chore was to draw water from the well for washing and cooking. I sometimes dreaded the mornings when it was my turn to lower a long, skinny bucket into the well in the icy dawn. The cold wet rope would make my hands hurt before I got the well bucket far enough out of the well to pull the lever. Dumping the water into a drinking pail, I trudged back to the house through the dew-soaked grass. We all used the same dipper and drank from the same pail of water.

I was not distressed by our move to the country. Leaving the small, gated compound was like being released from a prison. I loved the country, the wild animals, the woods, and just being distant from the city and the oily film of its harsh memories. There were more chores, but it was worth it. We boys took turns milking the cow early in the morning, stoking the coals and building a fire in the stove, and gathering eggs. We sawed enough wood in the fall to last through the winter. It was sometimes hard work, but, again, it was worth it being out of the city.

One cool morning, I went outside without my shoes on to draw a bucket of water. The cold dew and frost oozed from between my toes. But it was a beautiful ethereal dawn. As discomforting as it was, I enjoyed the pain of the cold on my toes, the frost biting my ears, and slight burning of chilled air in my lungs. I felt alive—washed in a wonderland of natural beauty. The sun sprayed its orange hue through light fog on the nearby peach orchard. The large grown-over garden was a sea of orangey glass. The frost-clad shrubs, broom sage, and dormant Bermuda grass glistened in shards of brilliant light. It was that period of dawn when the sun drove the waning winter's air to the ground.

I was about to lower the well bucket when the peaceful morning erupted in a burst of violence. The chickens and guineas squawked and screeched with alarm. I wheeled about just in time to see the tall grass waving furiously. It was over almost as quickly as it started. In an explosion of feathers, one of our turkeys succumbed to a predator. The culprit was most likely a fox or coyote.

11 years old

We didn't stay long in that small house. Mr. Willis built a new one next to the old shack we were living in. My brothers and I helped by holding the ends of ceiling and floor joists as he and another man nailed them in place. We also carried lumber, acted as go-fers, and cleaned up the job site. After Mr. Willis and his family moved into the new house, we moved into his old house several miles further into the country. It was a larger one than the one we moved out of, but we still did not have running water or an indoor toilet.

Being further out in the country suited me just fine. There were much more exciting and interesting things to do. The experiences, some good and some bad, caused me to appreciate living there. I learned how to make and shoot a bow and arrow. I set traps and caught wild game. One winter, I sold hides I had tanned by stretching and nailing them to the smokehouse wall. I also learned how to use a saw and hammer.

Mama and us boys worked for part of the rent. She helped Mr. Willis farm, harvest peaches from the large peach orchard, and pick produce from the truck patch. We sawed wood for the stoves in both houses, built fences, and did many other things together. We boys also helped by doing various jobs at Mr. Willis' new home where he owned a large acreage. I have a picture of Mr. Willis, Mama, and me standing in a field where I had helped to spring Bermuda grass.

It was a good friendship. Mr. Willis was probably in his late 70s when they met. He died in his 80s one summer day while under a car working on a clutch. Mama was handing him a bolt through the open floorboard when suddenly he didn't respond.

The family allowed us to continue living in the old house. However, the stigma of being different returned when I began attending my new school. For the next couple of years after we moved to the country, we went to school in the small town of Onapa. Someone put up a sign out on the highway identifying the town as "368 people and a few old grouches." The school was perhaps the only employer in the town.

I did not expect to be bullied in that school. In fact, I was initially excited and looking forward to a fresh start. My high expectations crash-landed on the first day. The Onapa school was a "bullying hell." It would not be unreasonable to believe that bullying was a school-sanctioned event. So many kids were involved in the bullying process that it might be easier to count the ones who were not involved.

I was not the only one who was bullied. One kid was tormented much worse than me. He had amblyopia, commonly known as "lazy eye." That single anomaly made him a target. Their bullying was brutal and almost constant. It appeared as an art form that the bullies, both male and female, believed they had a right to perform. Sometimes I felt great pity for him. However, and to my shame, on occasions, I was relieved he had drawn the attention away from me.

I think they initially picked on me because I was a new kid. Once a large group of students from different ages formed a circle about me and taunted me. One of them slipped behind me and got on his hands and knees. Another one attempted to push me. When I reacted by backing up, I tripped over the guy behind me and fell. They all laughed and jeered. I got up swinging, but there were too many of them. The main perpetrators were older than me and easily avoided my swinging fists.

The teachers never tried to stop the bullying. Perhaps they considered it to be harmless child's play. I supposed that a kid could have been severely beaten and no one would have come to his or her rescue. It was a small school, and most teachers may not have actually wanted to be there. It certainly seemed that way when I first met the basketball and P.E. coach, Mr. Grunden who appeared angry all the time.

In class one day, I felt the brunt of his anger. My classmates were passing around an old tennis shoe. I don't know where they got it or how the game started. I often would put a library book behind my textbook and read. Engrossed in my book, the noise of their laughter was in the background. Mr. Grunden was laughing too. I looked up as the shoe was passed to the guy next to me. When he passed it to me, I tossed it out the open window. It seemed logical to me. The shoe was dirty and stank. They had all quickly gotten rid of it. So I thought I was solving the problem.

The class went silent. It was as if I had broken something.

Mr. Grunden, eyes staring holes through me and voice dripping with scorn, asked, "Why did you do that?"

I knew I was in trouble. I didn't know exactly what to say that might ease the situation. Mr. Grunden had a reputation of being quick to grab the paddle.

"I thought it was a good thing to do," I replied.

"Well, did you think about what might have happened if someone were walking by?" He replied. "You could have hurt somebody."

I did not want to disagree with him, but I wondered who would be passing by since recess was over. Then he said, "Come up here."

He opened the desk drawer and pulled out the paddle. It was made out of a thick board, like a small boat paddle. He had drilled several holes in it.

I walked up to the front as he had commanded.

"Bend over that desk," he said, anger seething in his voice.

I bent over the desk and took fifteen blows with the paddle. The pain was near unbearable. The blows were so powerful that they slid me forward on the desk. I could feel the tears coming, but I held

them back. I stubbornly resisted giving him the pleasure of forcing me to cry out. Instead, anger rose up so powerful in me that I wanted to turn and punch him in the face.

When he quit, he said, "Now get back to your seat and see if you can stay out of trouble for the rest of the day."

I went home on the bus that day in great pain. After exiting the bus, I could barely walk up our graveled drive. Mama was standing outside and noticed right away that I was injured. She asked me what had happened, and I told her in detail. That was the first time I saw her angry on my behalf. She called the school principal. The next day she went to meet with the principal and teacher. Nothing was ever done about the incident.

I was even sorer the next morning, but I went to school anyway. I was determined to show Mr. Grunden that he had not defeated me. I had been paddled before, but with what looked like a ping-pong paddle. Several teachers spanked me with their hands. It was the first time I had been paddled with a board designed to cause as much pain as possible.

Some of the boys tried to add insult to injury. They taunted me at school and on the bus ride home. Mr. Grunden or someone had spread around that I was a complainer and a "sissy."

I was always very skinny and looked like a weakling, but that was not the case. During the summer, I worked very hard in the fields and the orchard. But I didn't know how to fight. So I had hung a burlap bag from a tree limb and packed it with more burlap sacks. I had seen boxing matches on television. For weeks after I hung the punching bag, every evening when I got home from school, I would beat on it until I was tired.

I also had become friends with a fellow named Johnny who was a couple of years older than me. He had two sets of boxing gloves. Like me, Johnny was spurned by the social order at school. We frequently sparred in his backyard. He taught me how to box defensively and offensively. I learned how to jab and punch, hook and uppercut, and to block and defend against punches. Johnny was bigger and older than me, but I was eventually able to hold my own with him.

One day, the kids began picking on me in the school bus on the way home. One kid took the lead and tried slapping me. I can remember his blonde hair, the smirk on his face, and his demeanor as he tried to intimidate me. His words were vulgar and very offensive. We began scuffling with a seat between us. The bus driver stopped the bus and let us get off and fight. It was something he often did when two guys got in a verbal or physical tussle.

The other kid was known as a fighter and very confident that he would defeat me. He was a guy that all the girls adored. I didn't like him because he was part of the social group that bullied me when I started school at Onapa. I also didn't like him because he was popular with the girls, and I was someone they all avoided. Finally, I didn't like him because he was so arrogant and confident.

When we began fighting, it didn't turn out as well as he expected. The bus driver didn't let it go on too long before he broke it up and told everyone to get back on the bus. The guy was very angry at being humiliated by a low-class boy in front of a busload of kids. He made a lot of threats but never followed through. From that day on, they knew I would not be bullied again.

When I was of age to begin high school, I had to register and attend school in Checotah again. It was different that time around.

14th Birthday

The other students seemed to be preoccupied with other activities including dating. I seldom encountered any bullying throughout the period I was in high school. Furthermore, no one gave me any grief on the long bus ride to and from school. It may have been partly because we caught the bus at the end of our driveway instead of the city dump. However, I still kept to myself as much as possible. I had a short fuse when someone attempted to dominate or ridicule me.

I do not mean to leave the impression that I was a courageous, tough guy. I didn't really want to fight because of fear that I would lose and be further humiliated. Except on rare occasions, I tried to avoid altercations. Additionally, I was by nature timid and didn't want to hurt anyone. But when I became fearful, or faced the certainty of unbearable humiliation from a bully, the rage erupted. It overpowered every other concern. Even then, if someone had had enough, I would let them walk away. I didn't have the "killer instinct." My goal in high school was to get through the day as uneventfully as possible and get home to my sanctuary in the country.

My life in the country also began to take on a more solitary paradigm. When school was out at the end of the day, and especially when it was out for the summer, I kept to myself most of the time. Every evening after school when it wasn't raining, I would grab my axe, and, followed by my dog Nicky, head to the woods. Wandering in the woods took me away from the frequent commotion in our household. The solitude helped me to push down some of the pain of rejection and inferiority. Then, I tried to layer over the hatred with imaginations and fantasies in my reordered and reclusive world.

Sometimes I became lost in my thoughts about ways to leave the area. It was an ever-present and driving force to get away. I wanted to go as far away as possible and never come back. There seemed to be but one way to accomplish that, and it was through music. I believed if I could just become a good enough guitar player and singer, I would find a way out of the poverty and shame.

CHAPTER 8

SEARCHING FOR ESCAPE

Sometime after we moved to the country, we ceased going to the same church together. I was relieved that Mama didn't make me go to hers anymore. I had quit going to Mama's church because of the memories, and in my opinion, the music was dull. Instead, I began going to a Pentecostal church. The guitars and other instruments besides the piano and organ attracted me. Also, many of their songs were up-tempo, and they let me play guitar with them. I had no desire for God or even to know about anything spiritual. My entire focus was on music.

With money I saved from pulling boles and chopping cotton, I bought my first guitar, a plastic one from Alden's Catalog. It had three steel strings and three plastic ones. Using the instruction booklet, I managed to tune it. The booklet also included a chord chart. After several weeks, I learned how to play a few basic chords and sing some of the familiar songs in the booklet.

Sometime later, I played an old metal body National guitar that one of our neighbors had. I loved that guitar, but he wouldn't part with it. I bought my first wooden one from the General Store at Onapa. It had a cowboy painted on the front. After that, I got an old archtop Harmony. At some point, I bought an electric guitar and an amp.

Playing guitar and singing became my obsession. Moving to the country, playing music, and my frequent escapades into my private world of imaginations and fantasies helped me to survive. I cursed and hated the people who were associated with the negative thoughts until hate became the major barrier. Sometimes, I would wander deep into the woods to be alone. All of it together constituted a fragile wall between the past and present. All the bad memories associated with the period were forced on the other side of the wall. When they spilled over to oppress me, I kept rising up in the strength of my hatred and pushed them back.

The paradigm worked okay until I reached full adolescence. When I turned fifteen years old, I began hoping I might have a girlfriend. However, I was very self-conscious and nervous around girls. The thought of rejection provoked such powerful anxiety that my mind and heart was impaled by it. When a group of guys and girls were laughing nearby, I often wondered if I was the subject of their laughter.

Wandering about in the woods one day, it dawned on me that nothing there could help me. There were trees, rabbits and squirrels, ticks, and I had to watch out for snakes, but nothing was going to make my status better. I decided that something had to change.

I fancied owning a car by the time I got my driver's license. My immediate goal was to somehow get a job. There were few jobs for teenagers except common labor that paid very little, but I intended to save my money. If I were going to get better clothes, I had to take whatever job was available. These things had to happen before I could find the courage to talk to a girl.

Besides owning a car, there was only one other way I could think of that might help me be accepted. Everyone admired and accepted the athletes, even the ones who were not from rich families. They wore jackets with the school mascot embroidered on, and each of them had a girlfriend. Some even had several pretty girls competing for them.

I decided to get involved in sports. I tried out and made it on the football team. But Mama wouldn't give the school her permission or pay the small amount for insurance. I begged Mama to make a way for me to play, but she refused. Even the coach tried to get her to change her mind. However, she was unyielding in her decision. I threatened to leave home and never come back. She threatened to whip me for talking back to her.

On Friday evening of the first game, I thought about what it might feel like to get on the bus and be with the team. Without Mama's permission and insurance, I would not be permitted to play, but I would get to travel with them. It was an away game. I could almost taste the excitement. The thought of going to another town to watch the team pit their skills against a rival team was intoxicating.

That Friday evening, I asked her to let me go with the team to the game. She refused. One of her rules was that unless we went to a church function or similar social event, we were not permitted to leave the house after dark. I had never wanted something so badly. It was too tormenting for me to remain inside, so I went outside. I decided to climb to the top of a tree in the front yard and hide there. It was an attempt to make Mama believe I had gone away. I wanted to see how she would respond.

When she noticed I was gone, she searched through the house for me. Then she opened the back door and called my name. I didn't answer. High in the tree, I felt gleeful satisfaction that I was causing her discomfort. Finally, she sent my brother to look for me outside, but he didn't see me hiding in the tree. I heard her threaten, "If that boy went to that football game, I'll beat his hide to pieces."

Upon hearing those words, I realized there was no way I would ever play football or any other sport. My plan to escape the dark fate of social outcast melted like chocolate on a hot sidewalk. So I climbed down from the tree and dejectedly went into the house.

"Where have you been?" she asked angrily. Her forehead was wrinkled, and I knew I was close to receiving a whipping.

Sullen and completely dejected, I refused to look at her.

"I had to go to the outhouse," I lied.

The outhouse was about fifty yards downhill. I believed that my brother had probably searched it, but I counted on him not to expose my lie. He knew very well what would happen if she discovered the truth. Thankfully, he never said anything. She walked away without another word.

I thought, *What did it matter if I lied?* I would lie a million times and then lie some more. As far as I was concerned, that night my fate was sealed. I reasoned repeatedly in my mind, *If only she would let me play sports, everything would be okay.* I didn't believe that Mama was concerned about my safety. Instead, I was certain she viewed me as everyone else did. I believed she had accepted her position in society, but I hated it with passion. She wanted me to stay in the comfortable rut of poverty and inferiority, but I wanted to break out. Finally, I believed she did not want me to rise above her status.

I felt as if I had been sewn inside the skin of a dead man. I

Mama, dressed for church

84

wanted to shout as loud as I could, "That's not who I am!" In my mind, Mama became the primary obstacle to me breaking out of the suffocating confinement. The cold reality was, there was nothing I could do about it at the time.

I fell into an abyss of self-pity, vengeance, and despair. I concluded that what was important to me did not matter to anyone. In fact, I did not believe that I mattered. I reasoned that if I did not matter, then I wasn't going to let anyone matter to me. In my battle to overcome the anguish, a weed of rebellion formed in me. I had lived in fear of Mama. However, my fear was waning considerably. I deeply felt that if I was forced to become something I was not, it would destroy me. Yet, I was becoming someone I never wanted to be. Thus, I bolted into adolescence with a lot of extra baggage.

The drop that made the cup run over fell after I remarked to another guy that I liked a very pretty girl. Her family was nearly as poor as mine but without the stigma that we had. The guy told someone else, and by the time it circulated, she heard that I called her my girlfriend. She was mercilessly teased about the rumor.

I was in the gym one afternoon for some special event. I heard a girl call my full name. When I turned around, she was standing on the bleacher seat with a frown on her face. Some of her friends were gathered around to watch the show. She denounced me with the most scathing rebuke imaginable. It was so thorough a denunciation that there was complete silence in the gym for a few seconds afterward.

Her words dropped into my brain like acid. I was totally devastated. My mind was on fire with shame, and my cheeks burned with embarrassment. It could not have been worse had I asked her for a date and she declined. Escaping the social ignominy would be impossible when word got out about her rebuke. The blistering shame rode me like a demon. I fought back with sullen and stubborn anger. I told guys she wasn't pretty anyway, and other lies.

Then, in solitude, I blamed everyone for the girl's rebuke and other painful experiences. I blamed them for all my faults, pain, failures, and everything else wrong in my life. As my bitterness grew, I gradually morphed from a self-conscious daydreaming boy to a hostile and sullen young man. I refused to recognize my contributions to my predicament, i.e., rebellion, rejecting God, unwillingness to mitigate my hatred, and holding grudges. Instead, I made them my rights.

I realized there was nothing I could do to eliminate the now-unbearable sense of worthlessness. But if it remained, I would be trampled to dust underfoot of society. Thus, I had to play the blame game and to replace the weak "me" with a strong "me." By sheer desperation, the core purpose of my feeble childish struggle to eject the inferiority was replaced by a goal to drown it in hatred and rebellion.

I declared war on society and on anyone who would try to suppress me. That included Mama, schoolteachers, classmates, and everyone else whose maltreatment I had experienced. I spread hatred on their memories. I used hatred to elevate me above them in my mind.

My bitterness and hatred gave birth to a reckless desire to do something bad—something that would shock people. I wanted to do something that would make them think about what they did to me—behavior so bad they would feel guilty. It would present a rhetorical question, "See what you did—see what your judging has caused me to be?" I wanted to just get it over with, cross the line, and become what I believed they thought I was. Then I would go far away. I would permanently close the door to any thought of them—wash them and everything else away with the past.

I vowed that when I became rich, I would rent a plane, fill it with cow manure, and fly over the Checotah on Saturday. I would dump manure all over downtown in revenge. I did not realize that vengeance doesn't repair anyone. It merely sweetens the cancer eating away at one's soul. Vengeance did not change anything in me.

Nevertheless, I began breaking all the moral threads that had restrained me. I rebelled against everything that had the appearance of good. I decided that good was weak. I did not attempt to resist badness. Instead, I surrendered to the desire to cheat, curse, lie, steal, smoke cigarettes, fight, and whatever made me bad. I decided that bad was strong.

The public "me" became belligerently independent; a deeper and furtive "me" remained inferior and with festering wounds. It became a battle to determine which part would win over the sum of me. Eventually, it was as if a foreign entity was changing me—something I could neither control nor get rid of.

I lost the battle in a single night the first time I became drunk. The effect of alcohol on my spirit was like magic to me. It made the pain go away, gave me boldness in social settings, and the ability to subdue the powerful inferiority. I wanted more of it—as much as I could get. It did not matter what form it arrived in, beer, wine, whiskey, store-bought or moonshine whiskey. I just wanted to get drunk. I still believed that everyone hated me. However, the real tragedy was that I had come to hate myself.

CHAPTER 9

ON MY OWN

I had my first drink of alcohol when I was fifteen years old. I was visiting two friends who lived a couple of miles from us. One evening when we were all playing cards, their dad gave me a glass of whiskey and coke. It was a strange experience when the whiskey began to take affect. I didn't get completely drunk, but I wanted more. He wouldn't give me more.

Mama kept a bottle of Port wine for her heart palpitations. When she had one of her heart "spells," she would drink a shot glass of Port and lie on the bed until it passed. I began drinking her Port. She eventually realized that the bottle was emptying too quickly, so she hid it. However, I found other ways to get alcohol. I had a taste and a buzz and wanted more.

One of my few friends, Ira, lived a couple of miles through the woods from our house. Ira was an older boy who was a full-blooded Indian. Ira and I were not exactly best friends. If they got the opportunity, his older brother Joe and he would cause me some grief.

I think deep inside they disliked white people. But we tolerated each other because neither of us had any other friends at the time.

Joe physically attacked me once. He was bigger and stronger than me so I was quickly pinned to the ground. He bent my wrist backward trying to make me concede defeat, but I refused. The pain was so great I wept, but my anger was greater. I thought he would ultimately break my wrist, but I remained defiant. Eventually, he let me up, and from that point on he and Ira respected me more.

Surprisingly, Mama permitted me to leave after dark to go coon hunting with Ira's dad, brother, and him. One of them would always come inside and ask her very nicely. Maybe she felt bad about not allowing me to play football. I didn't care about the reason; I just wanted to be out of the house and doing something exciting.

As time went on, Mama allowed me to spend the night with Ira. She didn't suspect anything could go wrong since she knew Ira's mother. However, his parents were not very strict. If he told them we were going hunting, we could stay out all night. Initially, when we took the dogs, we actually hunted. But at other times, we were up to no good.

During one unsuccessful hunting trip, we had built a fire and were sitting around it trying to keep warm. There was a large lake nearby. We had passed one of the lake homes a couple of miles back. It didn't appear as if anyone was at home. I don't remember exactly why, but we decided to burglarize the house.

My adrenalin was pumping as we approached the home. We threw several rocks at the house with some of them hitting the door. When there was no response from inside, we took courage, sneaked up to the house, pried open a window, and slithered inside.

After taking some fishing equipment, food, wine, and beer, we headed deep into the woods to enjoy our spoils. A good distance away from the house, we built a fire and celebrated. I basked in a sense of deep satisfaction as we ate the food and got drunk on the wine and beer. That night and for the first time, I didn't feel helpless against the stigma of society. It was as if I had discovered and exploited their weakness.

We came home early the next morning. His parents didn't say anything to us. Burglarizing the house had made me feel powerful. I did feel conviction in my conscience but suppressed it. The major battle was overcoming my fear of being caught. However, because of our success, we decided to come back another week to burglarize another house.

Me, Clarence, and Charles, around 1963

When we discovered that most of the houses were empty during the week, we went on a crime spree. On one occasion, we stole a significant amount of beer and wine. We became so drunk that we passed out in the woods that night. I walked home the next day, and Mama never suspected a thing.

The word got out that some homeowners were setting traps to catch the burglars, so we stopped. I wanted to be a bad guy, but I did not want to end up with a long term in reform school.

In the same year, I started stealing some of Mama's weight-loss pills. I later discovered they were Obedrine, a powerful amphetamine known on the street as "bird eggs." The speed made me feel powerful and invincible. After taking all of them, I went to the pharmacy and got a refill. The pharmacist told Mama, and I never got that opportunity again.

Another day, I was feeling angry and very cocky. I wanted to do something rebellious. It was probably the effects of withdrawal from the speed. I decided to go to town and look for a way to get into trouble. It was a predictable step on the path I was following.

I found the trouble I was looking for at the pool hall. I don't remember everything I was doing, but I was doing it because I was rebellious and defiant. Whatever the rules were hanging on the wall, I was breaking them. The old man who owned the pool hall, Curly, thought I was being too rowdy. When Curly confronted me, it quickly escalated into a physical altercation. The police arrived, and I was arrested before I could get far away. I spent my sixteenth birthday in jail for disorderly conduct and assault.

Although I was responsible for being in jail, I became depressed and very dark in spirit because my birthday came and went without anyone noticing. Mama talked to the District Attorney and managed to get me out of jail a couple of days later. Someone must have talked to Curly because he didn't press charges. However, I was banned from the pool hall, which was the only place for entertainment in town.

I thought Mama would try to whip me, but I was prepared to stand up to her. I was determined that no one was ever going to have authority over me again. She must have realized the change in me. I was no longer the timid and easily subdued boy I had been. I had a confident and almost domineering, condescending attitude.

I had become deeply bitter and self-destructive. Various adults tried to talk to me to get me to understand the consequences of my direction. I would listen in stony silence. When they were through, I walked away without responding. When I went back to school, I discovered that the news about my arrest had made the rounds. Some of the older guys made snide remarks, but basically everyone shunned me. That was fine with me if they all stayed away.

I had missed several days of school and had a lot of homework to catch up. But I didn't want to go to school. The desire was overpowering to leave Checotah, play music somewhere making money, get drunk, and get everything that came with that lifestyle. I was still too young and insecure to attempt that move. But it didn't stop me from fantasizing and from getting drunk and cranked up on speed at every opportunity.

16 years old

Shortly after I turned sixteen, I got my driver's license. I wanted a car very badly but didn't have the money to buy one. Mama had an old car, a 1947 Silver Streak Pontiac that had quit running. So she parked it under a tree and bought another car. I repeatedly begged her for it and was surprised when she said I could have it. Later on, I overheard her and Mr. Willis talking about the old car and me. Mr. Willis had been the one to convince her to let me have it. He believed I would never get it running and that working on it would keep me out of trouble.

Well, I managed to get it running again, but it didn't have good brakes, the transmission slipped, and it didn't have a tag. Finally, I got the brakes to work but had to pump them every time I wanted to slow down or stop. I couldn't correct the rest of the issues. However, I drove it up and down the dirt roads near our house.

One Saturday night, I drove over to Ira's house and picked him up. Then I drove to the old drive-in theater and picked up a couple more guys. They all piled into the old car, and we headed to the Porum Barn Dance. It was in Porum, Oklahoma, about twenty miles away driving the back roads and the furthest I had ever driven. I had to stay on the back roads because I still had not gotten a tag. In fact, Mama had not yet given me the title.

We managed to get some beer at the dance. One guy in our group got into an altercation. The other guy's group was larger, so we wisely decided to leave. We peeled out on the dirt road going out of Porum and headed toward Checotah. Not far down the road, one of the guys looked back and saw headlights approaching from the rear. We were certain it was the same guys.

I tried to speed up, but the transmission began slipping, and the old Pontiac would not go up Tater Hill in a forward gear. So I managed to turn the car around and back up the hill. Then, I turned back around and sped down the other side. We got up enough speed to put significant distance between us and the other car. I decided not to attempt going to Checotah with the transmission slipping so badly. So I dropped everyone off and took the back roads home.

Several days later, I was driving back from Ira's house when the brakes failed on a sharp curve. I tried to navigate the curve that bent the dirt road around our pasture, but I could not slow down, and the old heavy car slid sideways and crashed into a tree. Mr. Willis, towed the old car with his tractor the remaining half mile home. I never drove it again.

That summer, I got a job at a service station. The job subdued some of my anger and rebellion. I was making a decent income and doing something other than working in the hayfields. I saved my money and bought a '53 Mercury with baby moon hubcaps.

I started attending church again but only on Sunday nights and for no other reason than to play guitar in the church band. However, later that summer, Roy, who was several grades ahead of me, was putting together a band. He heard I was a guitar player and asked me to play lead guitar for him. I'm not certain why he asked me because I was not that good, but it was probably because no one else was available. Afterward, I didn't play as much on Sunday nights at the church.

Being in the band was an incredibly exciting experience. We practiced for hours in the front yard of James, the bass player. Though we were not very good, we were very enthusiastic. In fact, our singing, especially the harmonies, was better than our musicianship. However, such as it was, the neighbors and everyone who showed up to listen got a free show.

Sometime later, Roy got us a gig to play for a dance in an old building downtown. It was the first time I had played with a band in a professional capacity. The experience had a profound effect on me. I was finally making money doing what I loved. Visions of grandeur actually did flood my mind. Even though the band didn't last long, I clung to the belief that I could make a living playing music.

The '53 Mercury turned out to be a problem. It was always breaking down and used a lot of oil. I traded it and paid some extra for a '55 Ford. I wrecked it in a head-on collision on a gravel road in Onapa. A woman was teaching her son to drive when he got rattled and swerved onto the wrong side of the street. It happened so quickly that I didn't have time to get out of the way. I wasn't badly hurt, but the woman had a severe cut on her head.

The woman's insurance company paid me several hundred dollars for the damage to my car. It was more money than I had ever seen or held in my hand. I did not go back to work at the service station. One of the first things I bought was a guitar. I do not remember everything else I spent the money on, but I strutted around like Mr. Big-time. I bought food and drinks at the Dairy Queen for Ira and anyone pretending to be a friend. I discovered

that a number of people wanted to be my friend when I was spending money.

It did not take long for me to spend all of it. I should have invested in another car. Without a car, I was stuck in the country six miles from town, bored and restless. I wanted to be where something was going on, so I frequently walked or hitchhiked into town every Saturday. Because I did not have any money, no one paid any attention to me. I would hang out watching everyone else socializing, laughing, and having a good time then would walk home dejected. I had experienced the power of money to attract friends and the depression of realizing it only purchased fair-weather ones.

One particular Friday, I had a difficult day at school. Instead of being bullied by white guys, a group of black guys started berating me. One of them was "junk talking," and I replied with threats of violence. It escalated to the point that one of us would have to back off, or we were going to fight. Some white guys came to see what the commotion was about. I didn't want to appear as a coward, so we fought. During the conflict, he severely bit me on the chest. It was an ugly bite that broke the skin and turned blue.

I had begun carrying a long and slender, pearl-handled, flip-blade knife. I whipped it out, and that ended the struggle. The junk talk continued, but he backed away. I walked off to take care of my wound. After that incident, I avoided coming near any group of guys, black *or* white.

The following night after that fight, which was Saturday, Ira and I ended up riding around with some guys who had scored some moonshine. Someone suggested we rob a country store about five miles north of Checotah in the tiny town of Rentiesville, an all-black town of probably a little over a hundred people. The store was owned and operated by an old black woman they called Mama Laurie, who was also a bootlegger. Mama Laurie kept her moonshine in a back room.

One guy distracted her by pretending to want a jar of shine. The rest of us nearly emptied her small store of its merchandise. The car was so full of goods that we had difficulty finding a place to sit. But we quickly found a sitting place because Mama Laurie came out of the door with a large pistol and declared that she would shoot us. We spun out of the driveway throwing gravel off the back tires. Drunk and euphoric, we got caught stupidly trying to sell the goods to a black man, Sonny Scroggins, who had a nightclub in Checotah. He called the police, and we were arrested and taken to the county jail. I spent my seventeenth birthday in jail.

When I appeared before the judge, the old t-shirt I had on was torn in the fight I had had the day before. After we were arrested, I had torn it the rest of the way and tied it in a knot at the bottom. The bite on the upper left side of my chest was bruised purple and swollen. The judge looked down at me and burst into laughter. Although I was sentenced to time in the county jail, we got off on the more serious charges. The parents of one of the guys made restitution for the goods we had stolen. I don't remember how long I stayed in jail, but it wasn't more than a couple of months.

When I got out, I was agitated, unhappy, and on edge. The course I had chosen was leading me away from everything related to Mama and my childhood. I was determined to travel it as far as it took me. The driving force was anger and to be free to do whatever I wanted. I was feeling stronger with every escapade and moving further from the persona of the timid and tormented young boy I despised. I wanted to completely abolish my old personality and image. Convinced that people thought I was no good, I was determined to prove them right. I intended to act out the stigma branded in my mind.

When I went back to school, I realized the news of my caper had made the rounds. A larger and older guy said something offensive to me about my being in jail. I was on edge and looking for trouble. I immediately challenged him to meet me after school.

We fought that evening near a small store where all the school kids bought their snacks. News of the pending fight had spread, and a crowd showed up to watch the contest. The guy swung "haymakers," but I boxed him. Each time he stepped in to swing, I jabbed him in the face. Just as a male teacher arrived to break up the fight, the guy had had enough and was trying to back out of the conflict.

Little real damage occurred. However, the teacher, for whom I never had any respect, began berating me. He always disrespected me in class and had once paddled me for a minor offense. I defiantly told him we were not on school property so he needed to mind his own business. He promised he would get even with me when I came to school.

The next time I was in the teacher's class, he accused me of something, and I don't remember what it was. I wasn't guilty, but if I had been, it was not a capital offense.

"Come up here, Fisher," he demanded. I can still see his blonde crew cut, the baleful blue eyes, and what I interpreted to be a condescending smirk on his face.

I answered, "No. You are not going to paddle me."

"You come up here—now—or it's going to be worse!"

I picked up my books and walked out. As I left the building, I raised my middle finger in the international sign of ill will. I decided that no one would ever paddle me again. I was through with trying to be accepted in school. After several experiences with alcohol, drugs, playing music, being arrested, jail, and missing school, I no longer felt like a schoolboy.

I decided it was time to leave. And that was the end of school, of the bullying, and the fighting.

I made some money for the next several days hauling hay. Although I stopped by a pond and washed off every evening, I knew eventually that Mama would find out I had quit school. I think the school finally called her and asked where I was. When Mama discovered I had quit school, she angrily ordered me to return. But I had broken free from her control. At seventeen years old, I had become too big for her to discipline.

One day, she trapped me in the bedroom and said, "I'll teach you a lesson you'll never forget!"

When she raised her hand to hit me with the stick, I ripped it out of her hand. Then I broke it in two over my knee and threw the pieces on the floor. I cursed her. I called her vulgar names that no one should ever speak to any woman, especially a mother.

Then with hatred pouring from the deep, I said, "If you ever try to hit me again, I'll kill you!"

Shocked, she asked with her voice trembling, "Don't you love me?"

I shouted in her face, "No, I hate you."

Tears welled up in her eyes, but I was impervious to her pain. The hate and rage had overcome my rationale and sense of decency. I packed a few clothes in a bag and cursed aloud as I stormed out of the house. I cursed her, the house, the school, the town, and life as I angrily walked down the dirt road toward town. There was so much hatred and something like deep despair in me that I did not care what happened to me at that point. I didn't have a shred of insecurity or fear of leaving. I vowed I would never return.

I walked to Highway 69 and began hitchhiking and walking toward Checotah. It did not matter to me where I went as long as it was away from everything that reminded me of the past. It was summer time, and I was not about to spend it stuck in the country or wandering around in Checotah.

I discovered much later that after several days, Mama went to the sheriff's department and reported me as a runaway. I must not have been a priority because no one came looking for me. I do not believe she wanted me to come back home after what I had said. She was probably worried I might do something bad in my rage.

I ended up later that first day in Tulsa, Oklahoma. There, I went through a series of lessons in the school of hard knocks. Within a few days, I got a job at a grocery store as a bag boy and janitor. But I was an ignorant hick who couldn't even figure out the bus schedule. So I often walked the 36 blocks to work and back. Some days, I would hitchhike and get a ride part or all the way to Brookside Market or back to my room.

Several times, when I had to walk along the main thoroughfare, I had several brushes with bad looking characters who would have robbed me or worse. I avoided them by leaving the main street and running through residential neighborhoods.

I also became acquainted with some older guy who supplied me with beer and cigarettes. Most of my money was spent getting drunk on the weekends, so I was often broke before the next payday.

I didn't have a permanent place to stay. Since I traveled light, I moved around to different hotels and motels. Once I spent the night in a cheap motel room downtown. Before I went to bed, I propped a chair against the door for security. Late that night or early morning, I was awakened by the sound of someone trying to break in. In my best authoritative voice, I told whoever was on the other side of the door, "If you know what's good for you, you'd better get out of here!" Just being in the downtown district at night was dangerous. It was a difficult and harsh period. Several times, I came close to having to fight my way out of situations. One minute, I would be walking along in solitude and peace, and the next I would be in a threatening situation with someone. I realized I had to get out of downtown but didn't have the money or knowledge about how to do that.

It didn't take too long before reality invaded my determination to be away from home and on my own. I decided I needed to go back home, make some money, and be more prepared for the next time I would leave. I left Tulsa and hitchhiked to Muskogee and then hitchhiked to Checotah. Mama barely acknowledged me when I came home, and I didn't say anything to her. I just came in the house and acted like I belonged there. I don't know how she tolerated me after what I had said to her.

The following school year, I briefly went back to school with the class a year younger than me. However, I felt completely out of place. I think the younger kids viewed me as an oddity. None of them would speak to or acknowledge me in the slightest. I felt like a freak, so I quit for good. I didn't finish the first semester of the eleventh grade. I decided that school wasn't worth the effort.

There were few opportunities to make money in the area during that period. I was often completely broke. The urge to get drunk and party was so strong that I began forging checks. In those days, one could write a counter check. So I wrote counter checks on people I knew had money, forged their signatures, and cashed them. It wasn't long before I was arrested. I spent a much longer period in jail. On Sundays, people came to sing and preach to us, but I shut them out.

In the plea bargain, I was given the choice to go to a Reform School, or I could enter the Job Core. I had heard horror stories about Reform Schools, so I chose to join the Job Core. The Job Core was President Johnson's program to help poor young people get a GED and a job skill.

In the summer of 1966, I rode a bus to the Gary Job Core Center near San Marcos, Texas. The Job Core Center was a volatile mixture of races. The Federal government apparently had not given much thought or preparation to the potential of racial conflict. In fact, there was a theater on the former military base where the person in charge, one night, showed a racially charged movie, "Bright Victory," about two army buddies, one black and the other white, who were blinded by war. When the racism showed up in the movie, there was a loud verbal protest from the blacks and threats of violence. Most of the black guys walked out of the theater. Had they stayed to the end of the movie, they might have had a different reaction. Leaving the theater and making it back to the barracks was a very intense experience.

The black people were in one section of the Center, and Hispanics were in another section. However, I don't remember there being many white kids. I was the only white kid in my barrack. The Gary Job Core Center was a dangerous place for a white kid without a support group. The black and Hispanic groups frequently fought. A single white guy didn't have much chance of surviving. However, I became close friends with a black guy, Kenny, from near my hometown. He had been an all-state basketball player. We often went to the gym together to play basketball.

As long as I hung out with Kenny, I was safe. There were several times he and I had to stand against some black guys who were determined to beat me up. Even in class, I had to watch my back. One time, in the restroom, a black guy tried to stab me in the back with a pencil. There were many threats, but I managed to stay within eyesight of a teacher most of the time. The danger of imminent violence kept me on constant alert. Kenny didn't go to my class, so I had to be on full alert when going back to my barrack.

On one occasion, I stayed in the gym until after dark. At some point, Kenny left with another guy, and I had not noticed his departure. When I realized it had gotten dark outside, I was worried. I knew that walking back to my barrack would be dangerous, but there was no other option. I had not walked far when I passed a barrack that had the door open. It was a sweltering hot summer night. One black guy near the door saw me passing by and shouted to the others, "Hey, that cracker just called me a n____!"

I didn't wait until they came out. As soon as he shouted, I started running full speed. I was never a blazing fast runner, but I became one that evening. Fear and adrenalin propelled me to perform beyond my ability. A group of guys chased me nearly all the way to the barracks. Had I not gotten a head start on them, I have no doubt I would have been severely beaten and maybe killed.

I heard stories of that happening, but I do not know for certain if they were true.

Although I was fearful of what they might do, I had no animosity toward them. I was a country boy who had associated with black people and Indians much more than white people. However, to them, I was a symbol of bigotry, persecution, and injustice which they had suffered all their lives. Just as I was, they were fighting back against an image of something repulsive in their lives.

After finishing my stint in the Job Core, I managed to get my GED and learn a trade in sheet metal fabrication. I went to work for a metal fabricator in Muskogee, Oklahoma. I did not work long before they laid me off. I was going around talking to people more than I worked at my machine. The foreman warned me a couple of times, but I really didn't care if I was fired or not; thus, I was fired. Not long afterward, I got together with some other musicians and played several gigs including the barn dance in Porum, Oklahoma.

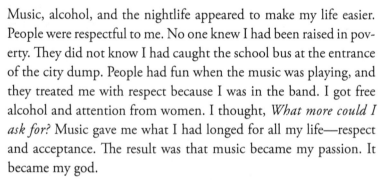

Music, alcohol, and the nightlife appeared to make my life easier. People were respectful to me. No one knew I had been raised in poverty. They did not know I had caught the school bus at the entrance of the city dump. People had fun when the music was playing, and they treated me with respect because I was in the band. I got free alcohol and attention from women. I thought, *What more could I ask for?* Music gave me what I had longed for all my life—respect and acceptance. The result was that music became my passion. It became my god.

During that time, I met another musician, Billy, who was a popular singer in the area. He gave me my first hit of marijuana. Billy usually kept several joints hidden in a Prince Albert smoking tobacco can. Since many people smoked hand-rolled cigarettes in those days, the guise was effective. Smoking pot provided another avenue of escape from reality.

I grew my hair long and began hanging out with other guys who smoked pot. I believe I was the first "hippie" in my hometown. During that period and region of the country, everyone wore short hair. One could look over the heads in any church congregation and see more crew cuts and flattops than any other style. There was strong opposition to the creeping invasion of the counterculture that had saturated the West Coast. My long hair was probably the reason I could not find a job.

The further I drifted into the culture of drugs, alcohol, and music, the more I changed. I quit searching for a job and spent all my time looking for people with whom I could get high or drunk. As a result, my personality was rapidly changing. I was being gradually swallowed by an underworld where weird didn't matter.

In that unreserved acceptance, I found peace. Little did I know, it was a false peace, and it was being provided at a price yet to be revealed. It was the brotherhood of broken lives, each with their own sad story. Each of them was running from something they could only escape and hide from in the darkness. I did not know or care that the darkness was not solving my problems but only obscuring them. The peace and acceptance I thought I had found was actually the anesthesia of deception on the highway to Hell.

CHAPTER 10

LIVING ON THE EDGE

Just when life appeared to be going along smoothly, one day Mama handed me a letter. It was a draft notice to appear for induction into the U.S. Army. I had turned 18, the draft age for all eligible young men. The war in Vietnam was pulling young men out of the country and sending them back in body bags. It seemed that every day there was a fresh body count in the news. Some of my classmates had been killed in Vietnam. I wanted to play music, get high, and have a good time. I did not want to die in a war I knew little about and cared nothing for. So I rushed down to the Air Force recruiting office and joined to keep from going to Vietnam as a soldier.

The military proved to be a maturing experience. I went through basic training at Lackland Air Force Base near San Antonio, Texas. That experience was demeaning and aroused heated anger in me. I was able to control it because I had to. Furthermore, I was with a group of other guys who were being treated the same way. A number of us became enraged by the rigid rules, humiliation, and the demeaning attitude of our drill instructor. We discussed tackling the D.I. and beating him up, but it never happened. We might not have been happy with the outcome had we confronted him. Most of those instructors were trained in hand-to-hand combat.

When I graduated from basic training, I was sent to tech school at Chanute Air Force Base in Rantoul, Illinois. After the discipline of six months of basic training, I felt like a prisoner set free. As long as I showed up for class, I could party until closing time at the NCO club, which was in our section and near my barracks. There were nights I got into a drinking contest to see who could gulp down a pitcher of beer the quickest. Some nights, I was barely able to navigate back to my barracks.

Although I did not like all the rules, it was very appealing to blend in with a group. We wore the same uniforms, lived in the same barracks, and no one was ridiculed about their past or social status. I was chosen as one of the leaders in the barracks, which required me to wear a green braided rope. For the first time in my life, I was given an honor. It inspired me to become even more independent.

However, I was chosen not because I had gone to leadership school as the rest of the leaders had done but because I had gotten into a fight after hours at the NCO club with several guys. Because I managed not to get pulverized, they believed I was a tough guy. All

In the Air Force pub—on right

the honor did was enforce my flawed view that good was weak and bad was strong.

The comradery, friendship, and absence of a scathingly brutal social stigma allowed my now developing narcissist personality to further emerge and grow. The more I got drunk, used vulgarity, and threatened violence, the more people seemed to respect me. No one dared to even hint at disrespecting me.

After graduating from tech school, I was given my first "leave" from the Air Force. I started drinking whiskey before I left the base and kept on drinking on the flight to Oklahoma. I did not immediately go home. Home reminded me too much of what I was trying to forget and destroy. I still had deep bitterness toward Mama. It drove me to reject and hurt her as I felt I had been rejected and hurt by her. I wanted her to recognize the deep pain in me and the fact I deemed her responsible. I wanted her to feel crushing guilt. So, instead of going home, I got off the bus in Tulsa and spent a couple of days drinking in various bars.

While in Tulsa, I ran into Earl, a guy I knew from a bar where I had played music. He invited me to go with him to Eufaula, Oklahoma where we went from one party to another. Eventually, we landed at a party in a mobile home behind a gas station. We were having a good time, and I had not been in a disagreement with anyone.

An older man named Bo was sitting to the right of me on the couch. He kept making disrespectful remarks about the military. At first, I laughed off his insults and focused on partying. At some point, I made the remark that there were guys in the military who could take him apart without trying hard.

Up to that point, all my fighting had been with guys near my age who were either not capable or did not have the nature to critically injure someone. Additionally, everyone mostly played by the rules. We did not hit people from behind, sucker punch anyone, et cetera.

Whenever two guys reached the point they decided to fight, they went outside and battled until one of them was defeated.

So I wasn't expecting any serious trouble from Bo. If he had challenged me, I would have invited him to take our grievances outside. One of us might end up with a busted lip, bloody nose, or black eye, and that would be the end of it. I did not realize I was in the room with a dangerous killer who had no scruples, a cowardly man who gained advantage by dirty tricks.

Suddenly, someone shouted, "Look out!" I wheeled my head about just in time to catch the strike from Bo on the left side of my head. He had wrapped a cloth around his hand, cupped a drink glass, and had intended to smash it on the front of my face. Had I not turned as fast as I did, it would no doubt have put out both of my eyes.

I never knew for certain why he did it. It was simply a brutal attack by a ruthless man who wanted to hurt a soldier. None of the words exchanged between us warranted such a vicious attack. He had hit me with everything he had.

I instinctively jumped up to keep from being trapped on the couch. The blood spurted out of my face onto the couch, the drapery, and the wall behind it. I stumbled to the door. I could hear people in the background trying to restrain him from continuing to attack me. I could feel his presence. I could hear his breathing. I heard people struggling with him very near my back. The storm door was locked, and I couldn't see clearly enough to unlock it. So I pounded it with several quick punches, shattering it to pieces. Kicking the rest of it out of the way, I staggered into the nearby service station. I sensed that Bo had backed off at some point. He was a coward and saw from the way I destroyed the storm door that I could still cause him some damage with my fists.

Cloney, one of my friends, was working that day. By this time, Bo had left the trailer and came after me. I am certain he meant to finish the job. Cloney asked me what had happened, and I told him. One of the guys in the station led me to the men's restroom to attempt to stop the bleeding. Bo showed up, and without saying a word, Cloney picked up a metal stool and knocked him back out the door. Seriously hurt and bleeding, Bo got in his pickup and left.

Earl came into the restroom and put a folded shop rag against the wound. He told me to press tight while he drove me to the doctor in Eufaula. The doctor was old, and his hands were shaking. He didn't want anything to do with me. My friend pointed out to him that I was in the military and convinced him to treat and bandage the wound. I had not taken off my uniform since I left Tulsa. The old doctor complied and then told them to take me to the hospital as quickly as possible.

I had lost a lot of blood and was trying to keep from passing out. The only thing I remember is pressing the rag against the blood-soaked bandage and Earl telling me repeatedly to stay awake. I ended up in the VA hospital over thirty miles away. I do not remember much about the trip or what happened when I arrived. There was a jagged and gaping gash in the left side of my face that required many stitches. They began a blood transfusion and put me to sleep to repair the damage.

During the several days I was there, Mama never came to visit me. Apparently, she was upset because the consensus was I had been drunk and disorderly. None of the hospital personnel, including the attending doctor, had a kind or encouraging word for me. Instead, they reproved me for being drunk and fighting. In their opinion, I was responsible for what had happened and needed to accept the consequences of my behavior. I was demoralized by their demeanor and felt completely defeated.

The attack had taken all the bravado and confidence out of me. I went back to being the timid and oppressed boy I had been all my young life. Even though I thought of responses to their remarks, I could not find the courage to say them. I had not been in a fight. I had been assaulted by a man I later learned had once killed someone.

Bo was someone who despised the military, in fact hated them and their involvement in Vietnam.

For me, I didn't even know there was an aggressive protest against the military. I was so sheltered in my hick world that I didn't keep up with current trends. If Bo was an organized part of that hatred, the military should have gone after him. Whatever his problem was, his intent was to blind me. Had I not gotten out of the mobile home, I would have probably been beaten senseless, bled out, and died.

However, no one asked me what had happened. Instead of being viewed as a victim, they treated me with cool apathy. When the old emotions I had blocked out returned, I felt guilty and believed I deserved the punishment. I meekly accepted their demeaning chastisement, but it did not stop me from becoming bitter toward Mama for not coming to visit me.

After I got out of the hospital, I went through a period of deep reflection. I thought of how I had been given leadership, of the respect people had shown me, and the other experiences that had boosted my self-esteem. I did not want to return to the weak and timid boy. I concluded that I had been on the right path. Bad was stronger—Bo had brutally proven that. Instead of remaining cowed and defeated by the experience, I became determined to be even more bad. I reasoned that my problem was that I needed to be bad enough that someone like Bo would never hurt me again.

I had horrible nightmares. When I was out in public, I scrutinized everyone, sized them up, and calculated what I would have to do to defeat them. However, the paranoia continued when I was alone. The term Post Traumatic Stress Disorder did not exist in that period. Later on in life, I took a self-test that proved positive for PTSD. To alleviate the symptoms that oppressed me, I self-medicated with drugs and alcohol. I had to be high to subdue the constant fear of an imminent attack.

I decided not to go back to the Air Force. The thought of returning and facing reprimand and possible punishment for something I didn't do was too much for me to bear. Equally compelling was that I had an overpowering desire for vengeance. It was my intent to kill the guy who had nearly killed me. I believed that if I killed Bo, I could remove the humiliation and reverse the loss of all my gains. I reasoned that killing him would push the inferiority and all the other baggage back to the box. Bo had stolen a part of me. The only way I knew to get it back was to kill him.

Bo had apparently left the area. Maybe he thought the military would come after him. I wanted to catch him alone in the right location and empty a .38 pistol into his body. My intent to kill him was a fixed obsession in my mind. I did not file charges against him with the local police because I did not want anyone to make him pay but me.

After a few weeks of sulking and plotting, I got some musicians together and began playing music as much as possible. We played music in every dive and beer joint that would allow us to play. Sometimes we played for tips and booze. Other times we split the door charge among us. When I was alone, I thought about killing Bo.

Eventually, I learned that Bo was known for sucker-punching people and other cowardly actions. Bo had hit another man from behind. While he was unconscious on the ground, Bo repeatedly drove over him with his pickup until he was dead. I was convinced I would not have survived had he trapped me in the mobile home or in the service station restroom that day.

After six months of being AWOL, I woke up one morning and my mind was clear. After lying in bed thinking about having to always be on the run, I realized I would never reach my goal of becoming a professional musician. Also my obsession to kill Bo began to dim when I realized what it was costing me. I decided to turn myself in to the authorities. I believed that if I pled my case in a military court, they might understand what happened. Although I still hated Bo and wanted him dead, I knew the chances of me being the one to do it were slim to none.

Several months earlier, a sheriff had almost caught me in a nightclub raid for underage drinkers. After letting me go, he had received a bulletin that said I was AWOL. He was former military and incensed that I had slipped away from him. He had put the word out that he was looking for me. I don't know my reasoning, but I decided to turn myself in to him.

I was held in the country jail at McAlister, Oklahoma until the military police came to escort me to Perrin Air Force base in Sherman-Denison, Texas. There, I was the only prisoner in the military brig. My time was spent reading and thinking about all that had happened. During that period, I renewed my aspiration of trying to become a professional musician. The battle against the bondage of misery and inferiority at times became overwhelming. I believed I might be sent to military prison and dishonorably discharged. If that occurred, I didn't see any other path in life for me but music. So I purposed that when I got out of prison, I would give my all to playing and singing.

A small squad of armed soldiers marched me to and from the mess hall each day. Everyone stared at me when I entered. It was very uncomfortable, but I kept my eyes focused ahead. I was embarrassed and felt totally worthless, but I was determined to get through the process and do whatever it took to settle the issue.

When it was over, I was court-martialed and stripped of my rank. The court had mercy on me because of the slashing I had endured and testimony by a psychiatrist. Thankfully, they did not sentence me to prison. Instead, they allowed me to remain on the base and apply my training.

After I was released to duty, I discovered I could have a good time in the Air Force. There was more liberty than I had when I was at tech school. It wasn't long before I was playing in a band on the weekends and drinking all the free beer I wanted.

Several months after I was court-martialed, Mama had a serious automobile accident which caused her to have a heart attack. I used that crisis to convince the Air Force to give me a hardship discharge to come home and help with the duties. At first, I fully intended to help Mama. The thought of her dying woke up some deep affection in me I did not know I had. However, when I saw she was okay, I had no desire to remain at home. I wanted to get out and pursue my goal of being a musician.

As soon as Mama was released by the doctor, I was out looking for other musicians and opportunities to play. I tried to get drunk as much and as often as I could. The scar on the side of my face was prominent. I was certain it made me look repulsive. The only way I could ignore it was to stay drunk or high.

I started gigging with a three-piece band and played each Friday and Saturday night in a nightclub outside of Eufaula, Oklahoma. It was a rough place where a fight could break out at any moment. The whiskey and beer were free for the band, so I left drunk every time I played.

One Saturday night, I left with Earl, the guy who had helped me in the restroom when I was bleeding. We went looking for something else to drink. After finding everything closed, we ended up driving to Tulsa. In Tulsa, we bought a couple of jars of moonshine and headed back home. On the way back, I became so drunk that I was getting nauseated, so I asked Earl to drive me home.

When we were about two or three miles from the house, I was about to throw up. I shouted, "Stop the car and let me out!"

It was winter, and a freezing drizzle was falling. Earl tried to talk me out of leaving the car, but I was adamant about it. We were at the top of a hill near Ira's Indian community. I got out of the car, awkwardly straddled and stepped over a barbed wire fence, and walked into the woods. When I got about fifty yards in, I laid down on the ground with my head on my arms. My mind was swimming, and I was very nauseous. At some point, I passed out. When I came to, my hair and clothes were covered with a thin layer of ice. I was still very drunk, but the dizziness and nausea had ceased. So I walked out of the woods and onto the dirt road. The road was very muddy, and the ruts were deep. The freezing rain continued to fall. I staggered along forcing myself to keep going until I finally reached Mama's house.

I could have and probably should have died of hypothermia that night. I erroneously figured it was the large amount of alcohol in my system that had kept me alive. When I woke up the next day, other than a bad headache, I had no harsh effects from that event.

Over time, our band went from gigging in the rough nightclub to playing in a state lodge on Eufaula Lake. It was an upscale nightclub and the nicest I had played in. One wall of the club adjoined the deep end of the swimming pool. Men would sit at the bar and watch the female swimmers. Each night, lodge guests would come in to drink and dance. On the weekends, some of the locals showed up.

I was shocked once when I saw two prominent members of a church I once attended, a man and his wife, come into the club. They were already tipsy when they arrived but too drunk to drive when they left. They had rented a room at the lodge, but they did not leave with each other. It fortified my belief that Christianity was not for me. However, I had met some good people in church. I wrongly judged the whole lot by the ones who were not faithful.

After that gig ended, I got together with another lead guitarist, Tim, and formed the Sour Mash Gaslight Blues Band. We played blues and rock, such as B.B. King and Steppenwolf. Gradually, we switched over to country music because we couldn't get work playing the blues. It was around that period that I changed my name to Cid. There were too many bad memories associated with "Cedric." For the rest of my music career, I went by Cid Fisher.

We needed a traveling vehicle, so we pooled our money and bought an old Chevy panel van. On the way to a gig from McAlister to Ardmore, Oklahoma (about 120 miles), the brakes went out. From that point, we didn't stop for red lights or stop signs in any other town we traveled through. Afterward, we got rid of the old panel and bought a hearse from a black funeral home director. I will never forget that he handed me a card with the inscription, "We're the last people in the world to let you down."

After a gig in Ardmore, Ralph, the drummer, was drunk and became arrogant. He made the mistake of challenging Tim. Tim hit him once, and that was enough. Ralph was bleeding from a gash over his eye. After stopping most of the bleeding in the bathroom, he wrapped himself in a sheet from the motel. When we began the long trip back to McAlister, Ralph crawled in back of the hearse and went to sleep.

Perhaps the only humorous part of this story is what occurred on the way back home. I do not mean to make light of the deep sin and wickedness I was in bondage to. However, it is part of the story:

We stopped at a truck stop to eat. Tim and I still had our suits and ties on that the gig required. While we were eating, one of the service station attendants rushed into the café with his face white with fear and asked, "Are you the guys driving that hearse?"

Tim, a man of few words, replied, "Yeah?"

The attendant replied, "Well, you need to come quick. That dead guy you had in the back is alive!"

Apparently, while he was refueling our hearse, Ralph had come out of the back still wrapped in the sheet. At the time the attendant was telling us this news, Ralph, still drunk and wrapped in the bloodstained sheet, staggered into the restaurant, walked over, and sat down next to me in the booth. We never told the attendant or the waitress that we were a band and that Ralph was our drummer. They treated us with extreme caution while we were in the restaurant.

Tim was somewhat of a practical joker and played it for all its worth. In his normal demeanor, he deadpanned numerous one liners about picking up dead bodies, et cetera. Ralph was not amused, but I fought valiantly to hold back the laughter.

Not long afterward, Tim wrecked the hearse, so we sold it to a salvage yard. I discovered later that some of the club owners had not hired us because of the hearse. Even the ones who did had us park it in the back of the club. Word had gotten around that we were a jinx and the club that hired us would lose customers. Not long after that, our band broke up because we couldn't get work.

Next, I joined with another guitarist and singer, Gene, and switched to playing bass. Our three-piece band began playing nightclubs in various nearby towns and cities. Gene was an older guy and a true professional. He not only knew how to get gigs, he knew how to work a crowd and keep them dancing. We were regulars at the same rough nightclub near Eufaula. The violence appeared to have gotten worse. There were sometimes several fights every Friday and Saturday night.

We also played at the Branding Iron in Fort Smith, Arkansas during the state fair and rodeo. The club was full of drunken cowboys and fair goers. The platform on which we played was encased in a wire cage to protect us from the violence. And there was plenty of it. One cowboy, Rocky, from my hometown got into a fight and was stabbed in the stomach. While he held his stomach, he beat the other guy senseless with the large buckle on his belt.

Sometimes, we had difficulty finding gigs. On several occasions, we went hungry. In one city, Gene and I broke into a permanently closed nightclub early on Sunday morning. The night was bitterly cold, and we needed a place to sleep. After spending the night, we robbed the vending machines for snacks and money. Somehow we managed to avoid being arrested.

In Lawton, Oklahoma, we played a better quality nightclub and made more money than we had previously earned. One night after the gig, we went to a party. Like Gene, I seldom took any drugs except speed. However, one of the guys at the party convinced me to take a hit of "blotter" acid. It was one of the most disturbing experiences of my young life. I cannot explain what the acid did to me other than to say I was transported into a surreal world of hallucinations.

It was a terrifying experience. I had no control over my body and mind. I was tormented by various oppressive emotions. When I reacted adversely to the trip, Gene took me back to the motel. Later that morning, I was sleeping and still high on the acid when some roofers began roofing the motel. I was instantly awakened by the noises. Heavily armed men with full battle gear had crashed through the wall and were heading toward me. Not recognizing it as a hallucination, I ran out of the motel room in my underwear screaming.

Gene ran out the door after me. While repeatedly telling me I was hallucinating, he grabbed my arm. He convinced me to let him lead me back into the room. On the way back, he cursed the roofers and demanded they stop working. Something changed in me at that point I cannot explain. The acid trip had done something to me psychologically. I quit the band and went home.

At home, I entered a period of solitude and deep reflection. The traumatic incident in the mobile home had changed me. Something had happened deep inside I could not understand. Some might label it a psychotic episode. Nearly every night, I had nightmares of people trying to hurt me. I developed a strong paranoia of people. Individuals who even hinted at being aggressive were kept at a distance. I never let a stranger get behind me. I eventually started carrying a gun and a large Buck knife, but the only way I could feel safe was to smoke pot, take drugs, and get drunk. I had been telling people for years I would die at forty years of age. However, at that point I did not believe I would make it that far.

CHAPTER 11

NASHVILLE

During that dark period, I did not want to be around anyone. For months, I lived in a small room that Mama had added on to the side of the house. I only spoke when Mama said something to me and then only as much as was needed. Occasionally, I went to town, sat alone on a bar stool, and drank a few beers. I still had some pot, so when I got back home, I would smoke a joint, play my guitar and harmonica, then sing and write songs until I got sleepy. I had become very focused and thoughtful about the desire to reach the top of my profession. At some point, I crossed a line. The only way I can describe it is that the "god" I had worshipped on the outside had come inside. I surrendered completely to the spirit of music as one would surrender to the love of a religion or a god.

After several months in my solitude, I got a gig playing in another lodge on Lake Eufaula. James, a guitar player from California whose mother worked in management at the lodge, was providing the music in the bar. He was looking for a bass player, and somehow we got connected. We hit it off instantly and became good friends. The job provided good wages for a weekend gig, but there remained a gnawing restlessness in me to make a significant move. I kept mentioning it to James until one day he randomly said, "Let's go to Nashville."

That's all it took for me to pack up and go. I had mentally cut all ties to everyone I knew. I felt like I was going into a new world, and I did not want them there. It was my "far away" world I had dreamed about for so long. Included in my dream were experiences, desires, and aspirations I did not wish to share with anyone, even James. In fact, I didn't want anyone to be so close to me that I could not abandon them at any time without saying a word. I didn't tell Mama or anyone else where I was going. I just disappeared, and I never intended to return. I wanted to be dead to everyone in my life that reminded me of the past.

Without thinking about how we were going to live, how much money we might need, and other important particulars, we loaded James' car that day and headed down I-40 toward Tennessee. It was a well-known fact that Nashville was full of very talented musicians, but I didn't care. I believed somehow I would make it.

When we reached Nashville, I was completely enamored with the nightlife. I felt alive, excited, as if anything could happen, and I had it all before me. My confidence was somewhat shaken when we went from bar to bar listening to musicians. The worst of them were better than anything I had ever heard. We asked numerous people if anyone needed a bass and guitar player. Most of them just laughed and replied, "Everyone's looking for a gig here." We didn't have any success that first night.

Getting a gig appeared to be a hopeless endeavor. We survived by not spending money on things we didn't need. That included enough beer to get drunk on. Each night we went to Demon's Den, owned by singer Nancy Dee. It was the bar where most of the musicians and stars came. We would each buy a beer and take a long time to drink it. That trick allowed us to stay in the bar so we would be available if anyone came in looking for musicians. If we emptied our bottles, the waitress would come by and ask us to buy another beer or leave.

Even with empty bottles, if there were plenty of empty seats on an off night, we were sometimes permitted to stay. Almost everyone including a waitress and possibly the bartender were looking for a break to stardom. So there was compassion until the place got full. Then the waitress would reluctantly tell us to either start drinking or move on.

During the day, we would come into the bar, buy another beer, and eat our fill of free popcorn. But the bartender and waitress knew that trick too. They had seen many starving musicians. Again, they were not completely heartless. They allowed us to get away with loafing and eating their popcorn to a certain extent.

Against James' protests, I put some quarters in the pinball machine. It appeared to me as the only way to get some money. I had never played pinball before and didn't know how to make it score. However, I watched other people play and witnessed a few of them win. Luckily, I won a game. It was enough money to get some beer and food with some left over. However, the next time I played, I lost nearly all the money I had left. I was convinced not to play it again.

One night in Demon's Den, James and I were nursing our beers and listening to the music. Occasionally, I got the opportunity to sit in with the band, sing, and play the bass. Afterward, someone bought us some beer, and we managed to stay until closing time. At some point, a guy who had been friendly to us came up to me and asked me to help him.

"There's going to be some trouble. Can you help me out with these guys? There's three of them against me and another guy," he said. His eyes had the wide-open look of someone on speed. He had been nice enough to buy us some beer, but I didn't want to get involved in his trouble.

I replied, "No, man, we're here to play music not fight."

I could tell he was upset that I refused to help, but he didn't argue with me. He hurried off to find someone else willing to fight. The band had just quit for the night, and there were only a few people left. The bar would be closing in a short while, but we wanted to remain as long as we could.

Just then, a guy ran in from the street and shouted, "There's a bad fight going on outside."

James said, "It might be that guy who tried to get us involved. Let's get out of here before we get trapped."

It sounded like a good idea to me. So we hurried outside intending to head back to the hotel. We exited the bar just in time to see the guy who had tried to enlist me in his conflict get shot in the stomach. He was shot a second time through his hand when he grabbed his stomach.

James and I tried to go back inside. However, we entered the door right into another conflict. The guy who had announced the fight was in a shoving match with the club owner's boyfriend, Bill. Suddenly, Bill pulled a pistol and shot the guy right above the right eye. As James and I watched in stunned disbelief, the guy fell on the floor right in front of us. His feet moved rapidly, kicking the legs of the pinball machine as if he was trying to run. Frozen in shock, we watched him kick out his life. He was the bus driver for one of the Opry stars whose name I can't mention. His mistake was agreeing to get involved in someone else's trouble.

We backed slowly out the door. James said, his voice shaking with fear, "Let's get out of here. Run!"

When we were completely outside, we turned and ran up Broadway. It was an uphill run all the way, and our lungs were hurting when we reached a peak. We stopped running at what appeared to be an old large church building. We sat down on the steps watching the people milling about below. It was surreal. Neither of us said much. We had just watched a man die, and we did not know about the one who was shot in the hand and stomach.

When the police arrived, we walked back down the street. The police did not permit us to get close to the scene, so we went to Linebaugh's café, an all-night café a short distance up Broadway near Demon's Den. We sat sipping cups of coffee loaded with cream and sugar and drinking refills until near dawn. The old chief cook, waiter, and bottle washer was as grouchy as they get. But he had a tiny soft spot in his heart for starving musicians. If business was slow, he would sometimes let us stay and drink his bad coffee.

We heard the next day that the guy who was shot inside the bar was DOA. Equally shocking was that we learned the newspapers had reported the incident as occurring in a café far from downtown Nashville. Someone remarked that it was because the city leaders did not want the tourists to be frightened away.

Later on, Bill (the man who shot the guy) befriended me after I once helped him string his Telecaster. I looked at his rugged face, his deep-set eyes, and wondered how he felt about killing the man. Bill's hands were shaking as he pulled the strings through the holes in the bridge of the guitar. I recognized the indicators of someone on speed. Bill had never had much to do with me before. We said "hi" in passing and occasionally chitchatted. Yet, he had gone out of his way to make certain I knew he was a friend. I wondered if he realized I saw him kill a man that night. Since I was standing right behind the guy, Bill could easily have shot me accidentally. I was neither questioned by the police nor summoned to testify. I heard much later that Bill had been found innocent by reason of self-defense.

With our small amount of cash getting very low, James and I still did not have a gig. It had been an eventful experience in Nashville, but it appeared we might have to find a job doing whatever was available to get gas for the trip home. We had rented a room in the basement of a hotel that was as bad as it gets. The room was in a row of rooms consisting of bare block walls and no ceilings. Once I saw a guy walking on top of the wall and peering into each room. I grabbed a stick I kept in the room and frowned at him. He quickly moved on, but it was difficult to sleep after that. We took turns sleeping and keeping guard.

The last day in the hotel, we had crackers and potted meat for our meal. Our circumstances looked dismal. I didn't know how we were going to get a gig. However, even though it looked like we were at the end of the line, I was not ready to give up. No matter how bleak the future seemed, the driving force inside of me was relentless.

The next night, now homeless and sleeping in the car, we were hanging around outside of Demon's Den. We didn't have the money for even one beer. A man named Lynn came outside and said rather loudly to several people standing nearby, "Anyone know a good guitar player and a drummer?"

James immediately called out, "Hey, we're looking for work."

Lynn came over to us. "Y'all pickers?"

James replied, "Yep. I play guitar, and he plays drums."

"Where you boys from?"

James replied, "Eufaula."

Lynn smiled and said, "Eufaula!" He stuck out his hand. "Y'all a couple Alabama boys."

I had no clue what he meant. I knew James had been living in Eufaula, Oklahoma, but I did not make the connection to Alabama. He hired us on the spot. Lynn was a steel guitar player for an unknown recording artist getting ready to go on tour. The hire was contingent on us trying out at the bandleader's house the following night. We discovered later that Lynn was from Eufaula, Alabama.

After Lynn departed, incredulous at what had occurred, I asked James, "What did you do that for? I can't play drums!"

He replied something to the effect, "Well, you're going to need to learn fast, or we're going to starve here."

I had only played drums while fooling around. But it was crunch time. I didn't know how I was going to do it, but I knew I had to somehow do well in that tryout. I had natural rhythm and had played with some country songs on the drums. So I ran over and over in my mind those past experiences, trying to remember what I had done.

That next day, after spending the night in the car, I hocked my bass and amp in a pawnshop. I bought a set of drums that I wasn't even sure how to set up. In fact, I had never put together a drum set. When we arrived for the tryout, I was relieved to see a set of drums ready to play. I adjusted the snare drum a bit higher and moved the bass drum a bit further away and said I was ready.

Jim, the bandleader, counted off a slow country ballad, the band started playing, and he began singing. I just hit a rim shot, kicked the bass drum on time, and tapped in time on the hi-hat. Jim was impressed. He said he didn't really want a fancy drummer, just one who would keep good time and not do a lot of rolls. That was a good thing because I didn't know how to do rolls.

We left the following night on a road tour covering several states beginning in Pennsylvania and ending up in South Dakota. James eventually told Lynn that we were from Eufaula, Oklahoma, but it didn't matter then. We had a job and were on our way to a gig. I figured I could fake my way through as long as the guy didn't do anything too complicated.

The night of our first stop was in a large nightclub in Lebanon, Pennsylvania. Surprisingly, he opened the show with a rock song country-style, "Proud Mary," and I was completely lost. I played so badly that Jim wanted to fire me immediately and continue the night without a drummer. There are no words to describe how panicked I became. He intended to hire a local drummer the next day to finish the gig. James talked him out of it and said I was just very tired. I think he told him we had been sleeping in the car and going hungry. Anyway, he won me a reprieve until the next night.

We got up the next morning very early and went to the club just as it opened for the cleaners. James had borrowed some money from the bandleader and got $20 of quarters. I sat behind the drums as he sat near the jukebox. He played repeatedly every song on the jukebox in Jim's repertoire. I played drums with the music until I nearly wore blisters on my hands.

Shortly before noon, they made us stop because they were opening for lunch. All the rest of the day, I had drums beating in my head. I know that I somewhat had learned how to play drums, and that night I saved my job with a decent performance. I did not know how to do anything fancy, but I could keep a solid beat. I had no trouble playing "Proud Mary" or anything else Jim chose to sing.

I practiced every day that week, learning to double kick the bass drum, play a waltz, and a bossa nova beat, and I could even execute some simple fills. A real drummer might have thought the word "execute" was appropriate for my playing.

At some point during the week, Lynn and I got into a poker game with the club owner and several of his friends. We were at the club owner's house, and he supplied everyone with whiskey. I had played poker before but never for money. Surprisingly, I began to win. Toward the end of the game, I had a large amount of cash in front of me. Lynn was also winning, but not quite as much until the final hand. He won more cash in that pot than I had won during the entire game.

Lynn said we had to go and prepare for that night's gig. However, the club owner insisted on playing one more hand. Lynn didn't want to, but the club owner wasn't smiling when he insisted.

We played another hand, and the pot had grown to a large amount of cash. Lynn had bet a significant amount in the pot. I had folded because my cards were not good. It was between Lynn and the club owner. In the final betting round, the club owner wrote on a piece of paper and said, "I'll call your bet with my nightclub."

The room was completely quiet. I could hear people breathing. Several more men had arrived. They were not playing but watching.

Lynn nodded his head. When the cards were turned over, Lynn lost. It was a very tense situation until that moment. After we left in Jim's Cadillac, I said to Lynn, "Man, you could have owned a nightclub!"

"Yep," he replied with his Alabama drawl, "But I wasn't about to win that pot."

"You mean you could have won it?" I asked, incredulously.

"Yep, but we wouldn't have made it out alive."

I stared at him trying to process what he had said. It dawned on me that he was a card shark.

"So, I had nothing to do with winning those pots, did I?"

"Nope." His one-word answer said it all. Lynn had made me look like the winner to take the focus off of him until he won that one big pot. The plan might have worked if we could have stopped when he sensed it was time to quit. I shared some of my winnings with Lynn since he had come out with much less than I did.

At the end of our last night, the club owner came up to Lynn and said, "Let's cut the deck—one time for a hundred dollars."

Lynn grinned and nodded yes. The club owner produced a sealed deck of round playing cards. I had never seen round cards. He took off the wrapper, shuffled them, and laid them on the bar.

"You first," Lynn said.

The club owner cut and turned up a jack of diamonds. A crowd had gathered. I thought Lynn would lose, but that didn't happen. He cut and turned up an ace of spades. The club owner laughed, then handed him a hundred-dollar bill. And then he said, "You're the luckiest man alive." It was evident he genuinely appreciated Lynn's talent. Lynn went on to become a steel guitar playing legend.

Toward the end of the week, one of Jim's friends, Charlie Louvin and his band, stopped by to listen to us. Charlie was a famous recording artist and a regular on the Grand Ole Opry, a historic

Nashville country music event. He was in town to play at the state fair. To my great surprise, he bragged about my drumming. He said it was difficult to find a drummer who would just keep a solid beat and leave off the fancy stuff.

After the tour, I returned to Nashville and wanted to begin playing bass again. However, I had become known as a drummer. When I would ask to sit in with the house band, the leader would announce that a drummer was going to play. Embarrassed, I would hurry to stop the drummer from leaving the stage. Then I would ask the bass player if I could play.

I have to admit, I never became an accomplished drummer. I lacked confidence and experience. If I had not been touring with a country singer who mostly sang ballads, I would never have pulled off the deception. So when one guy tried to hire me to play drums for a night, I managed to wiggle out. I had become friends with Peaches, a lady drummer who had stopped drumming because of an injury. The guy was a friend of hers. So she talked me into doing the gig anyway. I consented because I did not want to disappoint her. Her friend played all genres of music on that gig. That night, I was so terrified I drank several glasses of whiskey before the gig. I wanted to get drunk quickly so I could have an excuse for why I didn't play well. My friend, the lady drummer, was very angry with me over my bad performance. However, no one recognized that I was a charlatan.

Several nights later, I ran into Charlie in Demon's Den on Broad Street. He was looking for a drummer and insisted I go to work for him. Although I was not at all confident that I could handle the gig, I was somewhat drunk and was willing to do it. The opportunity was too good to pass up. Thus, after a short period in Nashville, I was playing drums for a country music legend. Later, I would play drum on the Grand Ole Opry. Back then, they did not have a full drum set on the Opry. There was only a snare drum, a hi-hat, and I believe there was a ride cymbal.

Charlie joined with Melba Montgomery to play the Old Plantation Music Park in Lakeland, Florida, which was owned by the legendary George Jones. That night, we were invited to George's home for dinner. George's wife, legendary country music star Tammy Wynette, prepared the dinner. Working with Charlie opened up many opportunities. I had acquired minor fame that I did not want to lose. I was known as the drummer for Charlie Louvin. Other musicians respected me. Further, I accessed an endless supply of drugs and alcohol. I did not care if I drowned in that river as long as I didn't have to go back to my old life of rejection, obscurity, and poverty.

I committed myself to learning how to play the drums better. At every opportunity, I sat behind the drums and played with the jukebox. Slingerland drum maker had given me a set of drums because I was playing for a star. There must have been a score or

Me (second from right) with Charlie Louvin's band

more of real drummers who wondered what had just happened. How did a low-talent performer get such a gig?

When I was in town, I hit all the hot sports. I learned about the backdoor of Tootsies. It was there I met another legendary steel guitar player, Jimmy, but I never got the opportunity to jam with him.

One week, during the D.J. Convention, I stayed up the entire week, night and day, taking free speed and drinking free beer. Once during the week, I became so wasted that I knew I had to eat. I opened a hamburger and crumbled some speed all over the patty. Then I forced myself to eat it.

At one point, Charlie and the band had to play live on a nationally televised program. The drummer who had been playing for the recording artists before us was Buddy Harman. Buddy was the top session drummer in Nashville. Because of his numerous

awards and playing on hit recordings, Buddy was already a legend at the time. Although I was drunk and speeding, I felt great anxiety flooding my mind. What little confidence I had was gone. I knew that Buddy would instantly recognize I was a fraud. But I had no choice but to attempt pulling off the deception again.

Buddy was left-handed. That meant I had to switch the drums to right handed during the commercial break and be ready to play. He was a very considerate individual and helped me switch the drums. Afterward, he graciously told me, "Good job!" I knew he was lying. Ashamed and embarrassed, I handed the drumsticks back to him and slunk away. I made up my mind to never again be caught in that type of situation.

I was in between road tours for Charlie and was in fact living in his home. Nevertheless, I began looking for work as a bass player. I knew I didn't have the talent and motivation to advance playing drums. Besides, I wanted to be up front of the stage. I missed playing and singing.

I purchased a great bass rig from a pawnshop. Every night, a house band played on Broad Street, so I played bass and jammed. There were some fantastic musicians. I watched bass players and learned how to play correctly. It wasn't long before I was becoming known as an accomplished bass player.

One night, Doug, another fantastic steel guitar player I had often jammed with, asked me if I wanted to go on a road gig playing bass with a popular singing group, the Four Guys. The Four Guys were the backup singers for the Grand Ole Opry and stars in their own right. After the road tour, I again played on the Grand Ole Opry with the Four Guys and that time playing bass.

Thus ended my short-lived drumming career. Slingerland got their drums back. The old set I had started on was long gone. It would be years before I sat behind the drums again and then only to fool around.

After the gig with the Four Guys, I went to work in Printer's Alley with the Curly Chalker Trio. Curly Chalker, a legendary jazz steel guitar player, was looking for a bass player. A friend and drummer for Mel Tillis recommended me. I auditioned for the gig, and Curly hired me after one song. It was a big boost to play in the Curly Chalker Trio as he was known for being very demanding to play for.

I did not stay long with Curly's group. Although it was a good gig, it was still working in a house band. I wanted to travel and to play with stars who might help me advance my goal.

I took a job with another recording artist, Doyle Holly, former bass player for Buck Owens. The guitar player in that group, Gene Price, was the former bass player for Merle Haggard. Both Doyle and Gene had won the ACM's Bass Player of the Year award. To play bass for them boosted my credibility as a bass player.

One of the stops on the tour was at the Cow Palace in Colorado Springs, Colorado near the end of July 1973. The Cow Palace was

Playing with Doyle Holly and Gene Price

the largest nightclub I had played to date. It had a large dance floor, and the place was nearly full of people every night.

When the band took a break, Doyle and most of the band members sat at a large table reserved for them. Doyle only allowed certain acquaintances in the circle, including several women, to hang out at the table. Sometimes, his fans came around to say "hi," but he made it clear they were not welcome to stay. Each night, a guy people called "Cowboy" tried to crash the small group, but one of the bouncers kept him away. He continued to come around when we took a break, hoping to be included. No one encouraged him, and he usually went on his way.

I seldom remained with Doyle, the band, and their small flock of admirers. My social awkwardness made me an unsuitable appendage to their party. For that reason, "Cowboy" homed in on me. I would lightly banter with him and then head to the bar. Sometimes, he was a bit difficult to shake, so I might turn away and acknowledge the first person within range.

On one Tuesday night, "Cowboy" was more persistent in getting my attention. He came up to me and said, "Look here. I want to show you something."

I had no interest in what he had to show me, but he was excited and very insistent. I could not think of how to excuse myself without offending him. So I decided to play along until I could make a smooth exit. He motioned for me to follow him so we moved under one of the spotlights glowing down on the dance floor. Gesturing for me to come closer, he spread open his shirt pocket and beckoned me to look inside. Inside, there were two pairs of ears, one pair black and the other white. I was stunned.

At first, I thought it was a prank. However, his maniacal wild eyes, goofy wide grin, barely restrained gleefulness, and splotches of what appeared to be blood on the bottom of his shirt pocket convinced me the ears were real. Immediately, my survival instinct went on full alert. With adrenalin pumping, I made a casual remark and diplomatically moved away. "Cowboy" snaked through the crowd presumably looking for someone else he could show his trophies to.

I was told later that "Cowboy," whose real name was Robert Lee Harpool, had picked up a sixteen-year-old black teen outside of a bar. Later, "Cowboy" and a couple friends picked up the boy's fifteen-year-old white girlfriend. They took the couple on a ride into the mountains. Somewhere along the way, "Cowboy" turned, shot, and killed them in the back seat. He cut off their ears then rolled their bodies over an embankment. That night in the Cow Palace was apparently the same night he had killed them. He was arrested early the next morning and charged with capital murder. The word was that he had been a patient in a mental hospital.

No one in the band appeared to be affected by the event. Two innocent young people were callously murdered, and no one around me expressed any signs of outrage or even sympathy. They brushed it off as the work of a madman and moved on. However, I had seen the evidence in "Cowboy's" shirt pocket of a brutal double murder. The embedded image of "Cowboy's" coldblooded act flushed my mind with fear and paranoia. It remained an intrusion in my alcohol and drug-sedated world. The image imposed the reality that malevolence wore many disguises, and in death, its victims knew no mercy.

For the rest of our time at the Cow Palace, I got drunk quicker and stayed drunk longer. Only when the whiskey numbed my nerves could I shake the ominous feeling that danger lurked in shadows and behind the cold eyes of a smiling face. I did not feel safe when I left the benign luminescence of the stage lights. Each night in the ebony shroud of the nightclub, I sat quietly at the table with Doyle and his noisy party.

CHAPTER 12

INTO THE ABYSS

W e finished the gig in Colorado and continued the tour with Doyle through Utah, then Albuquerque, and back to Nashville. While we were playing the gig in Albuquerque, I ran into Freddie, a friend I had met in Muskogee, Oklahoma. His drummer Ken and I bonded instantly. We hung out for a couple of days smoking pot and drinking beer before I had to leave for Nashville.

Doyle and I had several contentious arguments about the correct bass sound. He wanted me to put a sponge under the strings to produce more of an upright bass sound. Gene was okay with the way I was playing it. Eventually, I grew weary of him constantly trying to change my sound. When I got back to Nashville, I quit the group.

After leaving Doyle's band, I went on tour with Max Powell. Max had some success as a recording artist and more success as a songwriter. He was probably the legendary Webb Pierce's closest friend. I would often go with him to visit Webb in his office. On one occasion, Webb asked me to help him with a song. He also published one of my songs. An unknown singer recorded it, and it did not make him or me famous. However, after listening to several more of my songs, Webb said my writing had too much of a pop feel to interest Nashville publishers. He advised me to send a few to some publishers in New York City.

I remained with Max for several weeks of touring. He was easy to work for, and I got along with all the band members. However, when the tour finished and he didn't have any bookings in the near future, I knew I couldn't stay idle that long. So I got hired to play bass for an MGM recording artist, Walt Conklin. We went on tour through some northern and western states. We became snowbound in Mattapoisett, Massachusetts for over four weeks. It became very boring playing the same place for that long. Additionally, the customers had grown tired of us. There was hardly a night I didn't

Walt Conklin band (I am on the far left)

get completely high on speed and whiskey. Walt didn't mind how high I got as long as I did my job.

Faron Young, another country music legend, stopped in to see Walt one night. He tried to hire me away from Walt, but I wouldn't leave. I had heard that Young, who was also known as "the Singing Sheriff," had a habit of getting drunk and shooting his pistol. After the incident in Nashville, and my paranoia, I didn't want to risk being exposed to someone unpredictable and dangerous. So I turned down Young's offer and remained in Mattapoisett.

Walt designated me as band leader, and I took that job way too seriously. During that period, the drunkenness and drugs began to produce frequent fits of anger in me. It would just happen without warning. I didn't have any control over it, and it didn't take much to set me off. I had friction with some of the other band members. I was a perfectionist, and so I berated everyone (except Walt) who didn't play to suit me.

When the tour ended, I lived with Walt and his wife in New Jersey while playing gigs in the area. Sometimes during the day, I caught a train through Lincoln Tunnel to New York City. I went to a number of publishing companies to hawk my songs. Not one of them was interested. However, one publisher advised me to go to Nashville. I told him that a publisher in Nashville advised me to go to New York City. It appeared I was too pop for Nashville and too country for New York City.

While living with Walt, I played in Mack Sullivan's Rainbow's End nightclub in Woodridge. There I met and jammed with one of Walt's friends, Les Paul. Les was very friendly to me. Mack was a Hank Thompson fan and imitator, and the nightclub was famous for country music. However, when Les came to the club, I would talk him into jamming jazz and songs such as, "Back Home in Indiana." I also played at the Coral Bar in East Paterson. That was a rough joint and in a very bad neighborhood.

Taken during a solo gig in Florida

At some point, I decided Walt was not going to get back on tour soon, and since I didn't enjoy New Jersey, I decided to go back to Nashville. One day, without fanfare, I packed my stuff and left. I took a plane back to Music City and never looked back. Although Walt and I had been good friends, I had no reservations about moving on. In Nashville, I kept going from group to group, trying to position myself more in the spotlight and to keep moving up.

I went on a tour with another recording artist, Hal Wayne. He supplied a motorhome but always caught a flight back to Nashville. We had to drive the motorhome back to Nashville sometimes from across the nation. On one occasion, we detoured to Oklahoma so James could visit his mother and I could go home. We set up our equipment on Mama's front porch and jammed. I believe that was the first time Mama heard me play and sing after I became a professional.

When we returned to Nashville, I got a gig as front man for Sammi Smith, who had an epic hit song at the time. The gig was in Hot Springs, Arkansas during horse racing season. When we started the gig, Sammi was nowhere to be found. One of the guys informed me she would not arrive until the weekend. That meant I would be the only singer for the entire week. It was one of the best bands I had played with. It included Dickie Overby, another great steel guitarist, and the renowned fiddle player Ernie Reed. I played flattop guitar, something I had not done in a band before, and sang.

When the weekend rolled around, Sammi showed up with her husband, singer and great guitarist, Jody Payne. Jody took over as front man, and I was promptly dismissed and went back to Nashville where there were no gigs available. It was a let down to go from being with such a great group to being unemployed.

I was struggling financially when I was offered a house band gig in Chattanooga, Tennessee. I played bass and was the lead male vocalist. I hired Mike Chapel, a drummer I had met in Nashville, whose dad Don was once married to Tammy Wynette. I purposed to stay in Chattanooga until I had saved enough money to move back to Nashville without having to struggle to survive.

Although we were featured on a television show and drew large crowds, the music we were required to play was not my style. When the guitar player managed to convince the club owner to hire his girlfriend as a vocalist, it was not long before there was friction in the group. The main reason was because of my angry outbursts triggered by my whiskey drinking and having to play music I did not enjoy. I quit the band and went to work in the club as a bouncer and bartender. During the band breaks, I did a solo act: singing, playing the harmonica, and guitar. After regular hours, I worked in the lounge doing a solo gig for tips. By the time I started the after-hours gig, I would be so stoned I could barely play. Most everyone else was so stoned they didn't notice.

I went through a deep and dark battle with depression during that time. All my lofty goals had fallen to the ground. The bartending, bouncing, and solo gig were dead ends. I thought I would have made great progress by then, but I had no band; and it appeared as if I would have to slink back in defeat to Nashville and work as a sideman.

The old feelings of rejection and failure began to work in me. I had not reached my goal. The reality dawned on me that I was not polished enough for someone to finance my career. I didn't have the right personality and stage presence to be considered as a recording artist. In fact, unless I had several drinks, I could never quite overcome stage fright enough to even perform. Terrified that I would fall back to the bottom, I sought relief in the alcohol.

The nightclub owner, Randy, and I had become good friends. He offered me a room in a large house he had bought for his dad. His youngest brother, Mike, and another friend were also living there. I had also become friends with another brother, John, who was much closer to Randy's age. John often frequented the restaurant during the day. His son, Jim, also came for lunch, sometimes with his dad and at other times by himself.

Since Jim was a budding musician, I had conversations with him several times, but we never bonded. Jim had a melancholy spirit and was into dark music that I did not care for or purposely listen to. However, I noticed that Jim and his dad had a strained relationship.

One Saturday around noon, I came to the nightclub to eat lunch. I had spent the night at a woman's apartment and wanted some food and whiskey. When I entered the bar area, I noticed everyone was not as upbeat as usual. No one greeted or even acknowledged I had walked in. I stopped one of the waitresses and asked her what was going on. She told me that John had come home Friday evening, and there were satanic symbols sprayed all over the walls. He stormed to his son's bedroom to confront him.

When he opened the door, Jim was sitting in his bed, back against the wall, with headphones on listening to music (I think it was either Black Sabbath or Deep Purple). He shot his dad through the heart with a .306 deer rifle, killing him instantly. Then he put the rifle under his chin and pressed the trigger with his thumb. There was a great deal of shock and sadness in everyone for some time.

One night after drinking a significant amount of whiskey, I decided to also commit suicide. Although I had no desire to kill anyone, in my depression and drunkenness, Jim's solution to be free from his demons appealed to me. I did not see a way out of my bondage and failure. My drive to succeed was circumvented by deep acrimony, inferiority, and reality of failure. I felt I had failed and would never be anything other than a nightclub musician and a tormented drunkard.

After the gig that night (actually it was very early Sunday morning), I rented a motel room just down the street from the nightclub. After sitting on the edge of the bed, drinking whiskey and thinking about how confusing and bungled my life had been, I brought my pistol, a Charter Arms .38 caliber snub-nose, from under my shirt. I flipped the safety off, cocked the hammer all the way, and placed the end of the barrel against my right temple. My finger was tightening on the trigger. To this day, I am surprised it didn't fire. The trigger was sensitive, so it was easy to squeeze off a round.

After a few seconds, the thought came to my mind that the hollow point slug would probably take most of my head off. I don't know why—maybe it was raw vanity—but I thought that people would not recognize me, and I would die unknown. I eased the gun away from my head and using both hands lowered the hammer, and put it on the nightstand beside my bed.

I sat on the edge of the bed and drank more whiskey. Then I grabbed the pistol, took what was left of the whiskey, left the room, and got into my car. I was in no condition to drive, but I did not care. I headed away from the motel and toward some mountain roads. I decided to drive as fast as I could around the mountain curves until I had wrecked the car. Then it would all be over. Eventually, I lost control while speeding around a curve. The car flipped over and rolled down the side of a mountain slope. Bruised and shaken, I realized I was still alive. I crawled through a triangle-shaped opening where the windshield had been.

Making my way in the light of the moon, I climbed back up the slope. Then I somehow climbed up a mountainside to a home and knocked on the door. The people inside told me to go away and that they had called the police. Halfway back down, I found a rock shelf, sat down with my back against the mountain, and went to sleep.

I was awakened by sirens and saw flashing lights below me, surrounding the car I had wrecked. It appeared they were looking around with flashlights for a body, so I climbed down the mountain and walked up to the scene. A policeman quickly walked over and said, "Sorry sir, you need to leave the area."

I replied, "But that's my car. I'm the driver."

His eyes grew wide, and he shouted to the other officers to stop looking for a body.

I was taken to the police station, but they didn't put me in jail. Evidently, for me to be arrested for drunk driving, they had to catch me in the car. I received a ticket for reckless driving. After a couple of hours, they allowed me to take a cab home. I do not know what happened to the pistol. The police officers never mentioned it or the whiskey to me. It is possible that those items were thrown out of the car on impact or crushed under the metal during the wreck.

The next day, several people told me they were glad I hadn't died in the accident. I did not tell them I was trying to die. Later on, Mike went to where the car had been towed. He said the top was crushed in and the rest of the car was damaged beyond repair. "I don't know how you got out alive," he told me.

I had some bruises, including a very painful deep bruise, and some scratches, but nothing serious. The nightclub owner, Randy, felt sorry for me. He asked me if I wanted to go to Panama City, Florida for the winter and do solo gig in his other club. I took him up on the offer, but Florida wasn't the best place for me to recover from my depression. The city had a reputation for people coming from the surrounding states to party. They might be schoolteachers, possibly even Sunday School teachers, but they went wild when they came to Panama City.

I got drunk every night into the morning hours. However, the depression didn't go away, but got worse. I tried to commit suicide another time while in my car. Late one night, I was very drunk and driving from Fort Walton Beach toward Panama City. On one section of Highway 98, there was a long stretch of straight road. It was well after midnight, and I can't remember meeting another car. I pushed the gas pedal to the floorboard and held it there. My hands tightly gripping the wheel, teeth clinched, and staring at the white line that had become a blur, I braced for the next curve.

The car was going over 100 mph, but before I reached a curve, the engine blew. I abandoned the car and hitchhiked to Panama City.

On another occasion, I went into a bad nightclub one night with my pistol. I was looking for trouble and tried to start a fight. I didn't care what happened to me during that period.

At some point, the craziness and depression eased up. I went through another period of deep reflection and decided to go back to Nashville and try again. In Nashville, I made the rounds letting everyone know I was back. It wasn't long before I went out on a tour with lady recording artist, Martha Hall, through several states. We were in Athens, Georgia when I ran into Ken and Freddie again. They had been playing a gig in another club in Athens, and we met in a restaurant. Athens was at the end of the tour, and Martha was heading back to Nashville. So Ken and I decided to party. I got high for the first time on THC and some other drugs of which I never knew their names.

Martha Hall Band

I don't know how it happened, but after hundreds of miles and a lot of drugs and booze, I woke up from sleeping in the woods in front of Mama's house. Mama was surprised to see me when out of nowhere I walked through the door, but I was not very social. I sat around the house for several days wondering how I had made it back to where I started and how I was going to get out again. I wondered where my equipment was and where Ken had gone off to.

Over the next couple of days, I would wake up in the twin bed in the small extra room and wonder if I had dreamed all of these experiences. I had no equipment, no car, and no contact number for Ken, but I did have a significant amount of cash. If I didn't hear from Ken soon, I was prepared to go looking for him.

I was greatly relieved when the next day Ken drove up. He told me that at one point he woke up to discover the van was going over 100 mph, and I was sound asleep at the wheel.

We drove off to get high and talk about our adventure. I did not say anything to Mama. I left her again staring out the screen door as we sped off. I did not know I was going to submerge as deep into the counterculture with drugs as I had been in the country music scene of Nashville with alcohol and speed. Synthetic THC, marijuana, angel dust, MDA, Cocaine, Heroin, LSD, Mescaline, Methamphetamine, and all the popular drugs of that period would become my doorway to a narcotized world ordered by whatever I smoked or snorted up my nose. It was a surreal existence that allowed me to choose which tangibles of life to accept or reject. Subsequently, I accepted a different version of myself and cast the old one deep underneath clouds of hallucinations and delusions.

CHAPTER 13

ON THE DARK SIDE

I decided I was through with Nashville and its suffocating blanket of conformity. Instead, Ken and I formed a progressive and Outlaw Country band we called "Trigger Happy." We aspired to be the "cosmic cowboys" of Oklahoma. Outlaw Country music was challenging Nashville's long-held monopoly on country music. Waylon Jennings and Willie Nelson in Texas had revolted against the controlled Nashville establishment. Jerry Jeff Walker, The Nitty Gritty Dirt Band, Charlie Daniels, and other artists were inspirations that convinced me to flow with my own style of writing, singing, and playing music.

After our band played a few gigs, I didn't care if I ever went back to Nashville. I believed any path that bypassed Nashville would provide the artistic freedom to express myself. Conformity was never in my nature. I loved the fact that nothing in Outlaw Country resembled Nashville. The liberation gave me the motivation to begin writing songs again. This time it was without the motive of appealing to Nashville.

The music became an extension of the rebellion in me. It was all about fully expressing my wild and crazy spirit. Beer, pot, and the other drugs had replaced my hard whiskey drinking. There were times I had no clue what drug or mixture of drugs I was taking. Sometimes several guys would put their stash together on a mirror. One time, there was brown heroine, THC, meth powder, cocaine, mescaline, and PCP or angle dust in a pile on the mirror. Ken would use a single-edge razor blade to chop it into a fine powder. Then we would snort it for days, drink beer, and play music.

Ken and I also started dealing drugs. We bought pot by the kilos and speed by the 50,000 lots. I also grew pot behind the barn at Mama's house. I believe she was fearful of me during that period. I had grown a beard, carried a knife and gun, and had a persona that reflected how close I remained on the edge of violence. I treated her as if she did not exist.

Playing with Trigger Happy. My brother Clarence
(on left) was playing with the band at that time.

Our band became very popular in the area. With Danny and me on lead guitars, Ken on the drums, first Larry and then Jody on the bass, we had the Outlaw sound that was popular during that period. But the drug use kept us from doing anything with our success. Instead, we partied away the proceeds. One of our band members had a family, but he also loved to party; the party life eventually caused struggles in his household.

After a night of jamming and drinking beer in Muskogee, Oklahoma, I was headed to my apartment when a city policeman pulled me over. He did not frisk me but took me to the city jail. He asked me to take off my boots, which I did, and a bag of pot fell out. I was arrested. I knew someone had snitched on me. Ken was also stopped and arrested for having pot and a stolen pistol.

We were able to wiggle our way out of the trouble. I had a lawyer friend who helped me. However, there seemed to be "narcs" and snitches everywhere in Muskogee. I realized the volume of drugs passing through our hands was eventually going to get us in serious trouble. We decided to stop dealing in Muskogee.

I moved into Ken's house in the college town of Tahlequah, Oklahoma. We continued our all night partying and jamming. However, I had another brush with death in Tahlequah. After I stepped out to the parking lot of the popular Do Drop In club to smoke a joint, a guy shot at me. I heard or felt the velocity of the bullet as it passed by very close to my head. It ricocheted off a brick wall behind me. I went down low and moved between the cars in the parking lot until I could reenter the club.

After getting back into the club, I told Ken about the incident. We went out into the parking lot to take the guy down. Ken threw a brick at him to distract him. The brick missed and shattered the window of the car behind the guy. He was trying to reload a rifle when I came up behind him with another brick. Just as I was within striking distance, the parking lot began flooding with police vehicles.

I didn't press charges against the guy. It was not cool in those days to do business with the police. Besides, I had drugs on me. Once in the police station, they might have decided to search me. We chose to go back into the club and continued drinking.

Sometime afterward, Ken had a religious experience. For a period, he quit partying. He had eaten some Psilocybin mushrooms and claimed that God picked up the house and shook it. He said God told him to quit his lifestyle. He started hanging out with a preacher and reading the Bible.

One night, I invited him to drink some beer with me. We drank a lot of beer that night and got high. That was the end of Ken's religious experience but not his spiritual experiences. He went back to the mysticism and witchcraft. He believed in hobbits and reincarnation and insisted he had once been a wolf.

I didn't really know much about the devil at the time or his various religions. Although I had been raised in a Baptist church, I didn't know much about God either. However, sometimes we would get high and discuss spiritual things. During that period, I became deliberately involved with the demonic realm. That eventually led me to believing in spirits, reincarnation, and wearing charms and items I believed had magical power. I also became involved in cleromancy and I Ching and ancient Chinese Divinity.

Many strange things happened during that time. One night, Ken and another friend, Gary, went to a party at the house of a fellow named John, who was purported to be a high priest in the Church of Satan. They were sitting on the floor and sharing a joint with some other people. Suddenly, things began to rise off the floor, and a very strong evil presence came into the room.

Ken was so alarmed that he tried to pray. He could not remember the words to the Lord's Prayer, but he remembered he had a crucifix in his pocket. The chain that held it had broken earlier that day. He stuck his hand into the pocket and clasped it around the crucifix. Then he tried to pray again. Instead of the Lord's Prayer, he began whispering Psalm 23.

At that point, all the weird activity ceased. He opened his eyes, and everyone was staring at him. John cursed Ken and told him he had spoiled the party. Then he demanded that he leave the house.

"And take your _____ friend with you when you go!" he shouted.

Ken had almost forgotten about Gary. When he turned around, Gary was sitting with his back against the wall shaking violently. He was never the same after that. Whenever I saw him, he always had a distant look in his eyes as if he were in a trance. Although he would sometimes converse with me, if the conversation got slow or ceased, he would get that look in his eyes and go silent. One day in a local nightclub, he came up to me and said, "You've got to help me, Cid. They're tormenting me . . . I need help . . . they're coming for me."

I told him to just go drink a glass of beer. I really didn't know what else to tell him since at that time I had never heard of demon possession. I reasoned that he likely had a psychological problem. I had no inclination to help him, especially since I had enough troubles of my own to deal with.

A few nights later at Gary's apartment, we were sitting in a circle snorting some powder (angel dust, THC, or whatever) and drinking beer. A roaring sound began in the room. It appeared to be moving around the circle. Bottles started clinking together, and a chest of drawers rose off the floor. A couple of musicians were standing in deep conversation near the chest of drawers when it rose off the floor. The drawers began moving in and out.

One of them cried out, "What's going on!"

No one said anything. I heard them run out the door. I found out later that one of them had fallen down the stairs in his haste to leave and had been seriously injured.

The roaring sound became louder and seemed to be moving around our circle faster. The two bottles in front of me began rising off the floor as they clinked together. I could feel a strong fear rising up in me. As always, I responded to fear with anger. I erupted with an angry shout, "No!"

Everything instantly ceased at that point. I was no longer scared, but very angry. Something had occurred that I didn't know about or how to deal with. For some reason, we were all holding hands. I did not remember when that had occurred. To the left of me, Danny was squeezing my hand very hard. He was shaking violently with his eyes squeezed shut.

I jerked my hand free and said, "Stop. Snap out of it! Now!"

He quit shaking, opened his eyes, and asked, "What was that?"

Gary had that distant look in his eyes again. He was looking at me, but it appeared he was looking beyond me. He spoke as if an ancient sage, "I told you it was real." We did not know what had happened, but I knew it was something supernatural.

I met Gary one more time. It was right after I had made a trip to harvest some of my pot. I was growing some Panama Red marijuana behind Mama's barn. I didn't take the entire plant but only cut the buds off the tops. The buds were very rich in tetrahydrocannabinol, the active ingredient in marijuana. Gary came over to my place right after I arrived back in Tahlequah with the powerful pot. We smoked a bong pipe and sat quietly for a long period.

Out of the clear blue Gary said, "I know the Lord Jesus Christ is real."

His statement startled me. I looked at him for some sign that he was joking, but he was totally serious.

"Why did you say something crazy like that?" I asked.

He didn't say anything to me for what seemed like minutes. Then he turned and looked at me with vacuous eyes and said, "Because I've seen the other side." After that day, I never saw Gary.

Ken and I added another musician, Mark, making Trigger Happy a 5-piece band. We partied and jammed more than we got paying gigs. However, we landed a gig in a nightclub somewhere on the other side of the state. I cannot remember the name of the town, but I believe it was either in Tonkawa or Enid, Oklahoma. It was a full house the night we played. We were in the third or fourth set when the nightclub owner got into an altercation with a man. He pulled his pistol and intended to shoot him. However, someone hit his arm causing him to shoot right at the stage. The bullets buzzed by like mad bumblebees hitting the wall behind us.

Later after the gig, we were above the nightclub in an apartment where we were going to spend the night. The air was thick with pot smoke. We had drunk a lot of beer during the gig and still had a supply of beer left. Suddenly, pieces of wood started exploding off the floor. We were so high that we didn't understand at first what was happening. We were fascinated and leaned over to look at the holes. It appeared to me that bullets were coming through the floor, so I warned everyone to back off. Someone suggested that we put our amps and instruments under the bed and sit above them. Later we discovered that the nightclub owner had been shooting through the ceiling, which was also the apartment floor.

Not long after that, we moved back to Muskogee to play a steady gig in a new nightclub off Highway 69. Then a man showed up in town and began asking around about Ken. Ken told me he had made a huge mistake by getting some drugs from the guy for the purpose of dealing them. They were to split the profits. Instead, Ken sold or used all the drugs and spent the money partying. When the man came to collect, there was nothing left.

The man was a convicted murderer. In fact, we discovered later he was wanted for murder on the West Coast and was on the run. He could have killed Ken, but he would not have gotten his money back. So he decided to try to scare him into producing the cash. Neither Ken nor I had anything close to the amount of money he demanded.

A few nights later, we became very high on something, I don't remember what. I decided I would go to the nightclub where the man hung out and set him straight. I took my pistol in my boot and went to the place. Sure enough, he was sitting on a bar stool sipping a drink and talking to his friend, the club owner. I sat down beside him and began talking about Ken. I told him I would kill anyone who messed with my friend.

The club owner knew I carried a pistol. Neither of them were willing to risk being shot. I'm certain they slipped something into my drink because I felt the drug when it began to take effect. I had so much speed and other drugs in my system that it only began to make me feel drowsy. I never appeared affected enough by the drug for them to challenge me, and I decided to leave. It is a wonder the guy did not kill me.

After leaving the club, I drove along the back streets toward my apartment to avoid the risk of being stopped by the police. I could feel myself trying to drift into sleep, but I kept fighting it. Finally, the drug took full effect, and I fell asleep while driving down a street that dead ended at someone's home. The right front of my car hit a large oak tree in front of the house. The tail end whipped about and hit another massive oak. I don't know how fast I was going, but the car folded and jammed between the two trees. In fact, the frame pushed up the floorboard.

My head hit the windshield, but my felt Stetson hat somewhat softened the blow. However, I was cut severely enough on the forehead that it had to be stitched. I was taken to the hospital, treated, and released. I lost my car, but I had escaped two opportunities to lose my life that night.

Not long afterwards, I heard that a friend, Robert, had committed suicide. I had known him for a long time. We had sometimes partied together. The story was he had gone to a local church parsonage to talk to the pastor. He was high and deeply despondent. The pastor told him to go away and that he had called the police. Robert returned to his pickup, put a shotgun under his chin, and pulled the trigger.

Perhaps it was that news and my accident that shocked me to my senses. Our band was going nowhere. Although we were gigging, it was in small clubs and bars. The group was not progressing musically. I would set rehearsal times, but everyone would get high without fail before each rehearsal. Then, instead of rehearsing, we jammed. Then we would get even higher and drunker. At the end of the night, we had what we thought was a good time, but we never practiced. We had a lot of talent but would never rise above a mediocre bar and nightclub band.

The drive to excel in music would occasionally rise from the fog of our party life. I would talk earnestly with the guys the next day, but the cycle continued. With no car, and having made an enemy of a very bad character, I decided it was time to make a change. So one day, I told Ken and everyone I had enough. I packed up my equipment and headed to Tulsa.

Tulsa provided me a fresh location, but there were just as many people involved in drugs there as any other place. Many of the people who came to hear me play and sing gave me drugs. Initially, I took the speed and left the rest alone. However, I tried but I couldn't stop drinking beer and whiskey until I was drunk every night. I kept fighting to rise above it, but the lure of getting drunk and high always won out.

At one point, I got a gig playing bass with a Western Swing band in the Caravan Ball room. Most of them were former members of the Legendary Bob Wills Texas Playboys. They were great musicians, especially the guitar player, Eldon Shamblin. For a period, I managed to pull back the passion for getting high and drunk, and I worked very hard on my music. But Western Swing wasn't my style of music, so I moved on.

Next, I landed another gig playing weekends with a house band in a large restaurant and nightclub northwest of town. I was the lead singer and guitarist and the only band member who used drugs. My drinks and food were free, and I lived in one of the large apartments in the back of the club.

During that time, I signed a contract with a group of investors to produce an album. It inspired me to remain moderately sober. Additionally, a popular radio personality and his wife visited the nightclub regularly to listen to our band. They invited me on their radio program several times, which gave me more incentive to get the album finished. In preparation, I paid to have a number of my songs scored.

The recording session was a fiasco. Some of my old friends, including Ken, showed up. We got high, and they played on the album. No one showed up to produce it, so I produced it myself. That's a bit like someone being his own lawyer. The album involved a mixture of pop, jazz, folk, and Outlaw country music. It was impossible to identify a genre to label the album. The single that was released was also a waste. It had a hard Outlaw Country song on the A side, and on the B side, the title of the song was missing. The head of the investment group was in charge of getting the records made. He simply called it "Rock Song."

I became very discouraged when I realized I had wasted an opportunity. The result was to quit and run away as I always did when reality crept through the haze in my private world. I ventured from gig to gig, eventually working in a large motel in downtown Tulsa. During the week, the crowd was so low that the boredom was at times unbearable. I never played any of my songs. I quit in frustration, abandoned the investment group, and ignored the contract. A line in one of my songs, "Halo's are Hard to Come By," epitomized how I felt:

The desire of it all has passed,
In between me and nothingness,
There is nothing at all.

I began hanging out and often playing in George's Club, the West Tulsa nightclub frequented by a number of local musicians.

It was an escape from responsibility and reality. Like in Nashville, singers and band leaders occasionally came there to find musicians for road trips. George, the nightclub owner, was a dark-skinned guy with black wavy hair, a pencil mustache, and flashy grin. He loved musicians and gave me as much alcohol as I wanted when I jammed with the band. It did not take long before George and I became good friends. In fact, everyone that worked in the nightclub was like a family.

Harold, who was in charge of the music, seldom had to play his instrument. There were so many musicians coming around and wanting to jam that he just sat back and made certain everything flowed along smoothly. In fact, except for Harold on the bass and John the steel guitar player, I am not certain that George's Club had a house band. Harold and I also became good friends.

When I wasn't playing a paying gig, I was in George's playing in the jam session. Some of them in George's Club lasted into the early morning. George would close the nightclub at the appropriate hour, but Harold remained to keep watch on the booze and turn off the lights when the jam session ended. It ended when there were not enough sober musicians to keep it going. I often stayed up jamming and drinking until only Harold and I remained.

I was so consumed with drugs, alcohol, and music that I would remain high for days without food or water. I would crash for a couple of days and sleep for long periods. After I would wake up and eat, I would go right back into my routine. I went on a few road trips but stayed so high and drunk that most bands didn't rehire me. It was like my life in Nashville all over again, speeding and drinking whiskey to take the edge off and with no sense of direction. George's Club became my landing pad.

At one point, I boarded with an older woman named Elaine who was a practicing witch. She had a fondness for musicians. When she discovered I was homeless, she offered me a room rent-free in her house. Her witchcraft really didn't mean anything to me. Besides,

I stayed too high to notice what was going on. I was not physically attracted to her—it was just a place to live. Instead, I entered into a relationship with Sarah, a young woman who lived with her family across the street. She was also a witch, and her family was into the occult. Sarah appeared to be more into her craft than Elaine. I believe she may have been working some magic when her place was thick with the smoke of incense. I was drinking large amounts of alcohol and taking so much speed that most of the relationship is a blur in my memories.

During that time, I remained in a type of spiritual haze that I cannot describe. It was as if I was being led by something other than my own senses. I saw and did dark things including my brief involvement with Sarah. When she moved to Florida, I got involved with another young witch, Beth. In my somewhat sober moments it felt like Elaine, Sarah, and Beth were trying to draw me into whatever they were spiritually.

West Tulsa had an amoral atmosphere I felt was drawing me into its dark folds. Except for a thin bond, much like honor among thieves, not many of the people in the nightclub's "family" had any morality. Harold honored me as a friend and fellow musician, but he was otherwise without moral fiber. He had a nice house a good distance away but often lived for days in an apartment attached to the club.

One night, he was sitting in a chair with a large bottle that had a golf-ball size lump of pure methamphetamine, or perhaps crystal meth, soaking in some liquid. I did not know how he made the concoction. People lined up, mostly women, to let him shoot the mixture into their veins. He tried often to get me to try the needle, but I refused. I believed that if I ever shot dope, I would completely lose my soul. Furthermore, I knew if I ever allowed Harold to shoot me with dope, he would control me. So I declined each time he offered me the needle.

Harold had so much control over those needle junkies, both girls and guys, that they would do anything for him. I never saw him when he was not tripping on speed. The lower part of Harold's face, especially around his mouth, was deformed from a bizarre accident. No one really knows what occurred, but the result was that his lips appeared to be pursed together most of the time. His lower lip sagged so badly that he never closed his mouth. There were scars in that area of his face. He talked rapidly with a somewhat hoarse and low voice and could not enunciate some letters, such as "p" and "m."

That night, when all the addicts were satisfied and had left, I asked Harold how he could live so completely unrestrained. He answered my question with a story:

"I was a Christian once," he replied. He looked up knowing he would see shock on my face. He was right.

"*You* were a Christian?" I asked incredulously. "That's hard for me to believe."

Harold was sitting in a chair, leaning forward with legs spread apart and dangling the large bottle of speed mixture between them. He swirled the ball of speed around in the liquid as he talked. "Yah, and a preacher too." His head snapped about and eyes widened and bored into mine as if daring me to dispute him.

"A preacher? Man, how did you go from that to this place?"

"I preached with fire, and I put everything into it. I went around from one church to another—sleeping in barns and any place I could lay my head. It was a hard life, and I went hungry many times. One night, I was in a barn when an angel appeared. He said, 'Harold, you don't have to do it this way. You're trying too hard.'

"He let me know that all that preaching against sin was not necessary. I understood I had been suffering because I didn't understand something." He sat there as if waiting for me to prod the rest of the story out of him.

So I asked, "What was it Harold? What did the angel say that you were doing wrong?"

"He said that all God wanted was my commitment to him—that he didn't want me going around beatin' on people and trying to make myself right. He told me I was right enough, and nothing I did was going to make me any more right. That's what set me free."

I got up to leave. He took a swig from the bottle and said without looking at me, "You sure you don't want any?"

"No, I'm okay with what I got. I'll see you later Harold. I'm going in the club to get some beer." With that, I headed toward the door. At the door with my hand on the knob, I turned and looked back. Harold was sitting as he had been but with his neck bowed, head hanging down, and eyes fixated on the floor.

I was stunned by his story. Having been raised in a Baptist church, I knew on what he was trying to build his case. However, it appeared to me that Harold had taken that doctrine off its original rails and was riding it down the face of a steep slope ending in Hell. But I did not have enough knowledge to even know exactly how he went wrong much less how to straighten him out. I just knew somehow he had missed something somewhere along the way or that angel, which I doubted was God sent, would not have so easily convinced him to go bad. Of course, there was also the possibility that Harold was lying to me. He was so completely void of a conscience that I would never know if he was lying.

It was because of Harold's complete lack of morals that most of that period is unsuitable to recall and certainly inappropriate to write about. Hanging around him and living with witches did not leave me much room for a moral standard. Suffice it to say that satanic darkness will lower the human spirit to nearly the level of a beast concerning morality when drugs and alcohol are involved. Some of the musicians, groupies, and other individuals who hung around the nightclub were *very* spiritually filthy. *I* was spiritually filthy. I began searching for an exit to prevent "very" from being part of my status. There was much darkness in my life, and it seemed to be getting darker.

CHAPTER 14

BODY OF DEATH

One night, Billy, a good friend and a fiddle player, came by George's Club to jam. He told me about working a weekend gig in a small city northwest of Tulsa. He asked me to play one weekend, and I leaped at the opportunity to get out of Tulsa if even for a short while. The seediness of the club and the amoral people I was associating with had disturbed something deep inside.

The gig was like a breath of fresh air. A local farmer, Fred, played piano and was the leader of the group. I played guitar with them for several weekends. During that time, Fred and I became good friends. They were not great musicians, but being around them was refreshing.

One day, Fred told me he had a problem with some local thugs who had killed and butchered one of his cows. I remarked that someone ought to teach them a lesson. He offered to pay me to do the teaching. He invited me to stay in his house while I took care of his problem. Since there were several of them, I went back to Tulsa

In 1974, (I was 23) over twenty years after he left, my
dad returned for a visit. The first and only thing he said
to me was a negative remark about my long hair.

and hired a guy I knew who was 6' 5" and very scary looking. We called him "Lurch" in reference to Lurch on the Adams Family TV series. During a fight, someone had hit him between the eyes with a tire tool, and he never had the wound properly taken care of. It healed with a massive scar that was as fearful as it was unpleasant to look at. We had one fight with the thugs and scared all the rest into leaving the farmer's cattle alone.

After the situation concerning the farmer, I headed back to Tulsa. The only option I had was to return to the West Tulsa nightclub. However, I rented a room in the small trailer park right behind the nightclub. I was determined not to get caught up in Harold's wild partying and jam sessions. Instead, I went on a road tour up into Kansas and played in other nightclubs while in Tulsa.

Nevertheless, when I didn't have a gig, it became impossible for me to stay away from the nightclub. Gradually, I slipped back into jamming with Harold's group of musicians. Also, I had moved back in with Beth, the witch. I might have sunk back into the old paradigm if my good friends Ken and Freddie (not the farmer) had not walked in one night. They were headed down to Houston, Texas where Freddie had a well-paying gig in a large nightclub. They told me about how popular Outlaw Country was in Houston and asked if I wanted to go with them. I was excited at the chance to get out from having blundered onto a dead-end path.

Since they were leaving that night, I went to pack my things. Beth did not want me to go, but she knew it was going to happen.

There was one common thread I noticed in Elaine, Sarah, Beth, and even the nightclub owner George. When I manifested wicked behavior, whether it was a stream of vulgarity or I treated people with total disregard, they were obviously pleased.

"So you're going to load up and move, just like that?" Beth said, snapping her finger.

"Yes," I replied. "I've got to go. I need to be in Houston."

"What about me? Are you coming back?"

"I don't know. This is something I have to do—that I'm going to do."

She did not speak any magic words or burn any incense. Instead, she just stood watching as I packed up. I looked at her intending to say something more comforting, but surprisingly she did not seem sorrowful. Instead, there was a look of admiration on her face. It was as if she was impressed by my coldness, my utter selfishness and calloused disregard for her feelings. She just stood content with my decision, arms folded and staring at me.

"See you later," I said and walked out.

The driving force was awakened in me by Ken and Freddie's description of the music scene in Houston. I loaded my equipment in Ken's van and tossed my bag of clothes on top of the heap. In less than an hour, we were on the highway heading out of Tulsa.

The music scene in Houston was burgeoning with musicians. Many of them there were into alcohol and speed. Some professionals were calling Houston a viable alternative to Nashville. However, the music scene was more spread out than in Nashville. One had to travel from nightclub to nightclub to find a gig. There was no central place to gather and possibly land a job. Consequently, I initially had difficulty finding one.

For the first few weeks, I stayed with Ken in a house owned by a musician. He rented the spare bedrooms, but I had to sleep on the floor. I didn't have a car and had to depend on whoever was headed near where I needed to go each night. Just when I got a gig in a house band in Pasadena in the southern part of Houston, the girlfriend of the guy whose house I had been staying in demanded that all freeloaders had to leave. That meant I was homeless with only a few dollars, but I had a gig. I got Freddie to take me with my equipment to the job.

I played the gig that night and caught a ride to a restaurant that stayed open all night. I sat drinking coffee until after Freddie's wife went to work. Then I walked to Freddie's house. My boots had holes in the soles, so I put cardboard in them to protect my feet from the hot sidewalk. Freddie agreed to let me stay during the day, but I had to be gone before his wife came home from work. So I slept in a recliner in the living room until about 3 p.m. Then I took off walking to the bus stop. Freddie sometimes drove me to the nightclub where I stayed until it was time to play.

It was a harsh period until I got my first paycheck and was able to get a place to stay near the nightclub where I worked. When the money started coming, I began using drugs again, mostly speed. The nightclub gave the band free drinks, and I was already taking full advantage of that.

I played music for about five hours each night from Wednesday through Saturday. Each night consisted of taking a handful of meth tablets, drinking at least a half to a quart of Scotch whiskey, and smoking several joints outside the back door during breaks. After we quit playing for the night, I continued to drink whiskey until I passed out in bed. It was my way of coming down from the speed so I could sleep.

I used my old contacts in Oklahoma to receive and deal drugs. One guy, Joe, was actually a pharmaceutical salesman. He sold drugs to several musicians in the area. Some of the drugs were samples, and other ones were out of date. I was one of the few musicians at the time dealing, so he would bring me a significant amount. Included in the load were Dilaudid and Quaaludes, which I seldom took. There was also a significant amount of Percodan and some pharmaceutical amphetamines. Occasionally, I scored some "black mollies," a pharmaceutical amphetamine also known as L. A. Turnarounds. (Truckers claimed it was so powerful that if one took a "black molly," one could drive to L.A., turn around, and come back).

The most popular speed I took were white crosses, which were amphetamine or methamphetamine. However, there was no way to know what was in the tablets. They could have been made in the

USA, but many were made in Mexico. I would bag them up in 100 lots and sell them. However, a significant amount of powder was left over that I kept and snorted. I remember us rolling up a $100 bill and snorting two runs of powder, one up each nostril. Speed had become my staple drug. It allowed me to drink and party as long as anyone was available to party with me.

Each day, I would wake up around 1:00 to 2:00 pm, smoke several joints, drink a few beers, and start making the rounds from bar to bar selling speed. By the end of the day, I would be somewhat drunk. So I would go home, take a shower, eat, take several white crosses, and head to the nightclub to play. The next day, I started the whole cycle all over again.

While working at the Pasadena nightclub, I was approached by a songwriter and producer to record a single. That recording session was much different than the first one. Everything was done professionally. The single turned out great and began to get airplay around the nation. However, it caused friction between the bandleader and me. He also had a couple of records on the jukebox. Apparently, there was only room in the band for one recording artist, and it wasn't me.

I quit the band and joined Ken and Freddie to play in a large nightclub in Spring, Texas, north of Houston. Freddie also had a single record, but he never expressed a hint of jealousy toward me. Instead, he was always encouraging and a good friend. Billy Parker, the nation's most popular country music DJ, interviewed us both on the same night. The interviews were conducted and broadcasted live on KVOO in Tulsa, Oklahoma.

When I heard my record on the radio for the first time, I was ecstatic. My manager and I went on trips to radio stations to interview with program directors and DJs. I was always cranked up on speed and alcohol. When some called and told me they had heard the record in Oklahoma and that it was on the jukebox in my hometown, I felt like I had finally broken through the dark cloud.

However, instead of continuing to promote the record and being responsible enough to remain sober, I went on a long celebration high. There were times I left the nightclub so drunk and high on speed that I did not know where I was going. I often woke up in different places where I didn't remember how I had gotten there. We were fired from that gig because we could not draw a crowd. Our music suffered from the fact that so many key members of the band were high or nearly drunk before we even started playing. We were lazy, never practicing or learning new songs. We were basing our appeal solely on the fact that some of us had a record on the jukebox.

My manager tried to get me to focus on promoting the record. I would listen to him in the afternoon, but by 8 pm, I was in another zone. Other than occasionally going with him to a radio station to interview with the program director, I did very little. When I sat for a promo picture, it was not long after awakening in a drunken stupor from the night before, and it showed in the picture. My face was drained of color, there were dark areas around my eyes, and I appeared barely conscious.

I treated the record as if it were already a thing of the past. My plan was to celebrate for a while, then settle down to make a better record and perhaps an album. I thought I had broken through, but I was merely a small blip on the musical industry radar. Few people knew who I was, and fewer even cared. It was not often that I heard my song on a jukebox or the radio. No one asked me for an autograph. The whole affair was simply an opportunity I had not recognized and eventually wasted.

Freddie got a job in another large nightclub near the town of Bellaire, in the southwest section of Houston. He hired Ken and me and a piano player, Robbie. We took that job more seriously and set aside time for practicing and learning new songs. However, on Sundays, Ken, Robbie, and I would often get high together and run a string of nightclubs. If they were not with me, I would go by myself.

Sometimes, I mixed acid, mescaline, cocaine, and heroin, along with some powdered amphetamine. I would snort it and take some with me to snort when the high started wearing off. I would drink beer all day while snorting the mixture and swallowing meth tablets. By nightfall, I would be really crazy.

There was no predicting what I would do for kicks. One particular Sunday, I got really crazy. I don't know if it was because I realized I had wasted my opportunity with the record or if it was simply one of those times I wanted to self-destruct. That night, I went into a bar frequented by bikers and declared loudly, "I'll whip every S.O.B. in here!" Thankfully, because of the bartender, I did not get into a deadly altercation. The bartender talked several guys out of accepting my challenge and talked me into leaving. If the leader of the gang had been present, there was a strong possibility I would have died that night.

Some days afterward, I pulled onto the Pasadena Freeway and headed to Houston. Before getting far, my old Cadillac quit running, leaving me stranded in the right lane. Right then, there was scarcely any traffic on the six-lane freeway. I got out and raised the hood to see what I could do, not aware that the rush-hour traffic was sitting at a stoplight. The light turned green, and the flood of notoriously impatient drivers headed my way. I lowered the hood to witness seeing a cement truck barreling toward my car. I was frozen with fear with no option but to wait for the collision. The driver did an incredible job to avoid ramming my car. He stomped the brakes and turned sharply barely missing the rear bumper of my car. As the truck jumped the curb, it careened toward me balancing precariously on the left wheels. Dirt and other debris sprayed from the massive tires as it slid to a stop in a grassy area. The driver, terrified by the experience, backed the truck onto the road, parked behind my car, and said, "Let'em try hitting the back of that." Afterward, he helped

Promo photo for the record

me get my car started. If he had smashed into the rear of my car, I would have been seriously injured or killed.

Robbie and Ken had become good friends and did not always invite me to join their partying. However, one night they invited me to hang out with them. We got the crazy idea to steal some wine and beer from a convenience store. It was after hours, and the woman clerk told us she could not sell us any alcohol. I distracted the clerk while Ken and Robbie rolled a mop bucket full of booze out the door. I kissed the stunned female clerk and handed her some money. Then we took off like three dashing musketeers. Had we been arrested, we would have realized it was not one of our most clever ideas.

In the following weeks, I became so unpredictable that everyone refused to associate with me. Whenever we went out to eat, I often created a scene cursing and complaining about the quality of the food. Something had happened in my brain. I would go from having a good time and laughing in one second to instant rage at the slightest provocation. My unpredictable temper and violence had erupted so often that even Ken and Robbie refused to party with me.

One night, I became so enraged I nearly destroyed the mobile home I was living in. My girlfriend huddled in a corner as I beat holes in the walls with my fists. I also kicked large holes in the paneling and kicked doors off their hinges. My rage went on for what seemed like a long period. I could not even remember what set off my rage. My girlfriend wisely abandoned me.

When everyone left me, I was on nowhere street. I don't blame them for wanting nothing to do with me. However, when I was alone, I felt jealousy and anger toward Ken, Robbie, for the friendship between them, and of having girlfriends. I was jealous of Freddie for having a wife and home to go to. Everyone seemed to be happy but me, and I hated them for it. I was sure they were all against me and hated them for that also.

Somehow, I was able to keep my place in the band with Freddie. He never partied with us but went home to his wife every night, so he never saw the violent side of me. However, the spite and rage continued to foment inside. My diabolical narcissism had grown to maturity and was bearing fruit. It was the mental and spiritual condition that begets a murderer or induces suicide. I did not know God's law, and still I was trapped in a "body of death." I had lost control without becoming a needle baby. I desperately wanted deliverance, but had no hope that it would come.

CORRAL CLUB

Meet The Friend You Like To Meet

HOME OF...

TOMMY SCROGGINS-BAND

Featuring: Sid Fisher, Top Vocalist
Buck Jones, Guitar And
Bruce Ott on The Drums

Nov. 13, 1968

Court House Report

COUNTY CRIMINAL

Cedrick Fisher, Checo
Obtaining cash by bogus
pleaded not guilty; bond
$500.00.

Running stop si
ren, set January 15. Orville
warrant ordered issued. Erma
Reaves, warrant ordered issued.
Reckless driving—Gary Wayne
set January 15. Cedric Fisher, set M
19. Roger Dale Mason, $15 and cos
Following too closely—Lawson
burn, set December 26. Dennis
Lynch, set March 26.
Assault and battery—David
Meeks, dismissed. Paul Cobb, dismi
on motion of complaining witness.
cia Loraine Walker, dismissed. Ok
Lee Sumpxa, dismissed
Improper lane use—Valerie
McGeehon, found not guilty.
Petty larceny—Bobby Stilwell, 10
in jail. Thomas Ray Perry, $75 and co
Illegal exhaust—Ray
lord, $15 and

**Fisher Enliste
In U.S. Airforc**

Cedric H. Fisher, son
and Mrs. Samuel A Fis
Checotah enlisted in the
air force March 25.
Cedric attended Chec
High school and received
diploma from the Job Co
He enlisted in the mech
ical aptitude area and sco
in the higher 25 percent
the airman qualifying exam
nation.

174

CHAPTER 15

THE LAST CHANCE

Without Ken, Robbie, or anyone else to party with, I was forced to spend a lot of time in deep reflection and soul-searching. In desperation, I tried to cut back on the drugs and alcohol, but ended up drunk every night. It wasn't the usual out-of-control type of drunkenness, but it was drunkenness nonetheless.

My record was still playing locally at the time. I had tried to refocus on promoting it and cutting back on my addiction but kept sinking back into its grip. I had even become a vegetarian, started taking vitamins, and drinking raw juices. But whatever gains I made during the day with my healthy regimen, I lost that same night with the drugs and alcohol. Each day, I would start out smoking pot, and the high relieved the pain in my shredded emotional system. I would rationalize that I would feel even better if I drank a few beers. Once I had reached a certain level of "high," I free-fell into whatever else was available to get high on and imbibed to the max.

Consequently, my mood swings were so drastic I did not trust myself. I did not know or have any control over what I was going to do next. I went from raging anger and wanting to kill someone, even Ken, to deep depression and wanting to commit suicide. The diverse and large quantity of drugs together with the amount of alcohol consumption had no doubt destroyed my mind.

I could not blame my decrepit condition on Mama's harsh discipline, the bullying, the rejection, and poverty. Those memories and their pain had long ago been drowned in a sea of drugs and alcohol. At some point, the motive for my behavior became an egocentric quest for gratification. I was in that demonic bondage because I wanted the lures that drew me there. The lust for pleasure and accepting the lie of a false utopia was the bait I foolishly and callously accepted.

I tried to quit "cold turkey," but as in the past, I was a mass of raw nerves. I experienced indescribable torment and panic in my mind. It felt like I was going to explode, go crazy, go out of control, or completely lose my mind. The only thing that would make it go away was drugs and alcohol. I had reached the conclusion that I would never be free—that I would drink and use drugs until the addiction or something else killed me.

One Sunday night after the previous night of heavy drinking, I was sitting alone in the large nightclub where we played from Wednesday through Saturday. None of my friends were around. It had been a long time since I had gone all day without one drink. Fear had arrived with a hopeless feeling. It seemed as if I had fallen into a deep hole, and I wasn't going to come out. I believed I had gone past a point of no return, and it scared me. I felt like something very horrible was going to happen.

However, that particular Sunday night something different happened. I had been bothered for some time by something in my spirit but had tried to ignore it. It was something not noticeable when I was stoned. It was like a reoccurring urgent impression that

I needed to do something. It was as if I was being forced to consider the root of my drunken and drug-crazed rampages. But further than that, I was beginning to reflect on my spiritual condition.

I thought it was my conscience. I had seldom felt guilty about my actions, but now I felt guilt. I regretted the trouble I was causing and the dark thoughts in my mind. Other times I thought about God, about dying and going to Hell. I did not feel comfortable when those thoughts began to stir in my mind.

So, I was sitting there all alone, sober, and with ominous feeling, as if my conscience had awakened. I wondered if what I was feeling was withdrawal symptoms. I motioned to the waitress and ordered a glass of Scotch whiskey and some water. Then I said under my breath, "I wish whatever this is would quit bothering me."

Right then, I heard a voice speak. I was startled because no one was near me. Besides, the voice appeared to be in my head, but also in my ears.

The voice said, "If you want 'this' to quit bothering you, you must know that 'this' is my Holy Spirit. You're approaching the place where I can't reach you. If you want 'this' to quit bothering you, I'll never bother you again. All those times I kept you from dying. Yet, I won't be there when the next time comes. There will be no more chances to repent, to turn to Me, if you want 'this' to quit bothering you."

I sat stunned. Was I drunk? Was I losing my mind? I knew neither of these were the case. I had come to believe that God was just a myth. If I was sober enough, I often said the Lord's Prayer before I went to sleep at night. However, it wasn't because I actually believed, but mostly for luck—just in case I was wrong about God.

Somehow, I knew I was hearing the voice of God. I do not know how I knew that, I just knew. How can one explain such a thing? In the earthly realm, we used language to convey messages and communicate. Apparently, God does not have to do that, but can bypass our eardrums and deposit His message right into our souls as if we had heard it physically.

Immediately, I was taken back in my memories to the car accidents, the fights, the time I was shot at when leaving a nightclub and heard the bullet ricochet off a brick wall. I remembered the nightclub owner shooting through the bandstand and floor. I remembered the attempted suicides and all other near-death experiences.

God was telling me He had kept me from death. I thought, *God was there? He was protecting me? He was saving me from death? For what? If He is God, then He definitely doesn't need me.*

I was profoundly moved by what I had heard and was thinking and feeling. It was an indescribable experience. It felt like I had been dying in the desert and a drop of rain fell. Or as being locked for years in a foul, stinking prison with nothing but pig swill to eat, and someone asked if I wanted to be free. If all I had to do was say "yes" then I was never more prepared to do so. I replied, "I don't know who you are God. But if You want me, You can have me."

I knew I was no good to myself or anyone else because of the sordid condition I was in. I had finally made it up the ladder high enough to see the rungs at the top. But had the price been worth it? I couldn't quit the self-destructive addiction. I was completely helpless and did not have any options left.

That night, I did something I had not done in a long time. I went home without getting crazy high and drunk. I left the Scotch whiskey on the table untouched. The next day, I felt the ravages of withdrawal. I rationalized that the experience had been a hallucination in my damaged mind. The anxiousness and urging of my flesh and mind demanded satisfaction. I felt the urge to party drawing me to the lights—to get absorbed in the excitement of the crowd, the music, and the atmosphere of raw indulgence.

First, I smoked some joints and drank some beer. I felt a little uneasy, and I wondered if I might hear that Voice again. Within a few hours, I was back in the stream of "whiskey river."

All that week, I continued to drink and take speed, but I was not acting as crazy as I had been. Then the following Sunday evening after I had heard the Voice, I made plans to spend the night getting as high and drunk as possible. I sometimes hung out with a couple guys, Gene and A.T., who were bookies with whom I occasionally placed bets. Late that Sunday evening, I went to collect a large sum of money from them that I had won betting on football. I took half in cash and the other half in a significant amount of a powdered drug.

I met Ken later that night and snorted some of the powder. The stuff was extremely powerful, and we got very high. We got into my old Cadillac and headed down the Houston freeway at a high rate of speed. I was too high to drive, which was rare, so Ken was driving. We were so high that we did not care what happened. Ken sped down the off ramps, ran red lights, and raced back up the on ramp and back onto the freeway again.

We ended up in Ken's old friend David's apartment. David was an accomplished musician and great songwriter. The drugs that the bookies had given me were so powerful that everyone was very high, but I continued to snort the stuff. There was no way of knowing what type of drug it was. All I knew was that it was white powder in a baggie, and it made me high.

David, Ken, another guitar player, and I were sitting on the floor playing music. We drank a lot of beer, and I continued snorting the powder. Eventually, I took so much that I passed out. I very seldom passed out when doing drugs unless I intended to go to bed. This time, it was different. David tried to wake me up so I could leave. He did not want anyone remaining in his apartment after the party. Apparently, I had overdosed and could not be awakened.

The rest of my friends made it through the night okay. However, the next morning I was running a very high fever and was delirious. Somehow, I ended up on the couch. I am certain I did not get there by my own power. I assume David and Ken must have moved me there from the floor.

For almost three weeks, I laid on a couch in David's apartment going in and out of delirium. Even though we were not well acquainted at the time, David graciously allowed me to stay without any pressure to leave. I sweated so much I lost over thirty pounds. At times, I crawled into the kitchen and pulled myself up by the countertop to drink water. I didn't eat anything during that period. David would come home, and if I were awake, he would ask me how I was doing.

Then one morning, I woke up, and the fever was gone. I felt very weak, but I felt so good I could hardly believe it. It had been a long time since I had felt that good. I didn't even want food at that point. I got off the couch and went outside. It was a beautiful day. I walked barefoot to my car and got some clean clothing. I was stinking because of all the sweating and not bathing for nearly three weeks. So I took a long shower, changed clothes, and went back into the living room. I plopped down on a beanbag and thought, *I wonder where I could get some money and drugs for tonight.*

Immediately I heard the Voice speak again. He said, "Now your mind is clear and your body clean. Do you still want to surrender to Me?"

Again, I was completely stunned. I had not had a drink or any drugs in almost three weeks. There is no doubt that I had almost died. I knew I wasn't going crazy because I felt as clear-minded as I had ever been. I sat there for what seemed like a long time, and then I said, "Yes, God. If You still want me, I will surrender to You. But, I don't know how to do it. I need You to show me how."

There was no answer. I sat there reflecting on what I had heard and my reply. I thought, *What is He going to do? Why didn't He answer me?* I was never to hear that Voice in that exact way again. Yet some strange and remarkable things occurred afterward.

I went out and got something to eat. Early that night, my friends Ken and David came in. They were glad and expressed relief that I was well. David told me he and Ken were going to play a gig in Lufkin, Texas and invited me to come along. Although he really didn't need another musician, he graciously invited me so I could pick up some cash and get back into the flow. I briefly wondered if God would approve, but I really needed the cash and was very grateful for the opportunity.

In Lufkin, I had a motel room by myself. After playing the first night, I was sitting alone in the room reflecting on what the Voice had said. During the gig, I had only drunk a few beers and did not take any drugs. I felt impressed to read the Bible, so I looked in the drawer of a dresser expecting to find one. Surprisingly, there was no Bible in the drawer, so I lay awake for a long period thinking about everything that had transpired the past few weeks. I wondered, *Did God really speak to me, or had I gone over the edge? Have I finally damaged my mind with all the alcohol and drugs?*

However, it wasn't normal for me to be sober when I had access to alcohol. David had brought some pot and cocaine with him to Lufkin. But I was only interested in pursuing what new path God was taking me on and in finding what He intended to do with me. Something was happening to me I didn't understand, but I eagerly waited for God to show me what to do next.

The next day, I made my way to a bookstore and bought a Bible. I told the clerk I wanted a Bible without any of "man's stuff added." She asked me what I meant. I managed to explain well enough that I was referring to notes in margins. The only Bible they had without notes was a cheap one. It was large, thick, and had large type with the words of Christ in green.

After the gig that night, I could hardly wait to get back to the room and begin reading it. I decided to read the last part first. I wanted to see how it ended before I read such a thick book. I made it to the end of the third chapter of Revelation where it says,

"Behold, I stand at the door, and knock: if any man hear my voice, and open the door, I will come in to him, and will sup with him, and he with me" (vs. 3:20).

As I read the words, I understood what He was saying in that verse. I understood "sup" to mean supper. We had always called the evening meal, supper, in our family. I understood that He wanted to be friends with me. Somehow, I knew He wanted to come inside of me—that I had to let Him in just as you would open a door to someone who's knocking. I do not know why I knelt by my bed or said what I did. Maybe it was the Sunday School lessons or preaching I had heard many years previous. At that moment, I wondered, *What does Jesus want with me? What good am I to God? Even if He would accept me, this would never work out.* All my life, I was always starting but never finishing anything. I had usually quit and moved on whenever I became bored, was under pressure, or was facing failure.

None of that seemed to matter. All I could think of was that I had to try. My life had been one long journey toward self-destruction. I had tried so many times to break the pattern and failed. This was completely different. Something strange was happening, but it somehow felt right.

I got down on my knees and said, "I want You to come inside of me, Lord; be my God. I give you myself, and I'll do whatever You want me to do."

It felt like a huge weight just lifted off me and that I was encased (the best way I can describe it) in a huge bubble of love. It was the first time I had felt love or like I *was* loved. There are no adjectives that can adequately relate it as I experienced it. The pain and worthlessness, and all the other burdens I had carried for so long—all of it was gone in an instant. The hatred and vengeance in my heart also departed. Something was pulling the inside of me. I felt myself letting go of everything and just falling in total surrender to whatever it was.

I could not believe the joy and the peace. It was such a magnificent and deep feeling, so indescribable that what I have written here is as nothing in comparison. It was an instant change. I didn't want any alcohol or drugs but only to remain in that euphoria forever. If death would have brought me closer to the source of that beautiful love, I would gladly have died right then.

I don't know when I went to sleep that night, but I slept in peace. It was the first peaceful, drug and alcohol-free sleep in years. I cannot help but weep right now from thinking about that blessed experience.

The next morning, I went to meet the rest of the band for breakfast. Only Ken and David showed up. The first thing they noticed was that I seemed different. Ken asked me, "Hey, what have you been doing (meaning drugs)? Have you been holding out on us?"

I said, "It's not what you think, Ken. I believe I became a Christian last night. I just know I am changed somehow, and it's the best thing that has ever happened to me."

Needless to say, they were completely freaked out by what I said and seemed perplexed about how to answer me. On the other side of the table from them sat a man who had been totally committed to debauchery and selfishness. My vulgarity was legendary. There was seldom a decent word in my vocabulary. If I could replace a decent word with a vulgar one, I did so. Now I was clear headed and clear eyed. No vulgarity came from my mouth. The old vile nature was gone and my new nature glowed.

I played in the band that night, but my heart was not in it. We left Lufkin after the gig and headed back to Houston. I still did not know exactly what to expect next. I started reading the Old Testament in my Bible but did not understand everything I was reading. Needing money and a place to live, once again, I took a job playing lead guitar in Freddie's band.

Not completely understanding what had happened to me, I did not know what to do and where to go. In addition, I did not know a preacher or another Christian. Therefore, I just kept on working at my craft and waiting on the next step to manifest itself. However, the music did not mean anything to me.

We played a mixture of old and current songs. When it was my turn to sing, I did not want to sing one of the "cheating, heartbreak, adulterous, drunk, and hopeless" songs that typified country music. I wanted to sing something religious but did not know the words to one religious song. So I sang, "The Devil shivered in his sleeping Bag" by Willie Nelson. I changed a few of the words, but it was still not something one would sing in a church meeting.

I knew one thing for sure; there was something or someone inside of me guiding me. When I took a drink of beer, I felt emptiness in my spirit. I sat the beer down and refused to drink any more. When I inhaled from a joint of pot, I experienced the same feeling. Therefore, I gave the pot away. If I had known then what I know now, I would have flushed it down the toilet.

When I woke up in the morning, I did not drink a beer or smoke pot. Instead, I went outside and sat in a lawn chair. The beauty of the trees, the sky, the flowers, and the various birds hopping about and chirping fascinated me. I felt the morning breeze in my face, and my heart swelled with the exhilaration of freedom from the old bondage.

Each day, I went to various places searching for someone who could give me spiritual direction. I met a Guru in a health food store who called himself Darwa. When I told him what had happened to me, he tried to draw me into his religion. It didn't feel right to me, so I left. For the first time in my life, Mormons came to my door. They wanted me to watch a video, but that didn't feel right either. My brother Charles was in a cult in Houston at the time. I called him, and he set up a meeting with one of the leaders. After talking to him, I attended one of their meetings. They used the Bible, but again it didn't feel right to me. I bought a book on Transcendental Meditation, but only read a small part of it.

I had been praying and asking God what to do, how to get out of the music business, and how to totally break out of the life I was in. But, even with the lack of answers and not knowing what to do, I remained sober. I didn't want to drink or take drugs. Maybe it was a testing period I had to go through. It was an easy test as far as alcohol and drugs were concerned because I had absolutely no desire for any of it. But I wanted to know what to do next. I had some important questions, and I really wanted to talk to someone who could answer them.

Over the next several weeks, I fought with the temptation to go back into the music business. It was all I knew. I was running out of money and going from one cheap motel to another. It was evident I would eventually have to do something different. I'm certain some of my friends believed I had finally gone insane. To morph from a violent manic depressive and unpredictable man in one day into a Bible-thumper the next was no doubt to them inexplicable and unsettling.

Then one night, I had an extraordinary dream. In the dream, I was taken to the houses and apartments of the various people I knew and thought were my friends. They were not happy I had become a Christian. Some were mocking me, and others were saying they were going to stay away from me. The bookies I had gotten the bag of powder from talked about killing me to keep me quiet about the drug connection. A.T. and his friend Gene in the dream were going to take me for a ride, slit my throat, and throw me in the bayou.

When I woke up, the Voice spoke to me again, but not as before. I can only describe it as if the Voice had gone deep inside of me affecting both subconscious and conscious mind. The message was to fully surrender and let Him lead me. He told me I would have to trust Him—that He would have to lead me like a puppet. He said He would not do again for me what He was going to do this one time. I understood it was a special thing He was going to do with me. I slipped out of bed, got down on my knees and prayed. I wanted to be ready when the time came for His leading to begin.

Although I had fully surrendered to God in Lufkin, I realized this time I had to yield something more. The only way I can describe it is that I gave Him the control room—what I later came to know as my decision-making abilities. Instead of Him speaking and me hearing and obeying, I understood that He was going to do that differently. Instead, He was going to directly control me. Upon understanding that, I yielded my will completely to Him.

A few nights later, I called Mama. She was shocked to hear from me. I told her God had saved and delivered me from bondage. For the first time in my life, I told her I loved her. She replied, "Well . . ." It didn't bother me. After all I had said and done to her, she was right to be skeptical. I said I was coming home, and she said, "Okay."

If I had been in her place, I would have been apprehensive. But I believed that when we met, she would understand that what had happened to me was real. When I hung up, I wept tears of joy that I could truly love my Mama. But it was more than that. It was the fact that I finally knew love, possessed love, and could emit love from my core.

I cannot tell you how or why, except to say that all of a sudden everything seemed to fall in place. It was a quick series of events. I did not think about what I did, and there was no fear of ramifications. First, I told Freddie I was leaving the group. During a band break, I asked to speak with him privately. We sat in my old 1963 Chevy that I had sold my Cadillac to purchase. He tried to comfort and console me as if he thought I was upset about something. When he asked me why I wanted to quit, I reached into the glove compartment and pulled out my Bible. Holding it up in my hand I said, "Because of this, Freddie." He was shocked but only said he wished me the best.

The fact is that Freddie thought I had gone crazy and told everyone so. The nightclub owner, Phil, invited me into his office to talk me out of quitting. I told him the story of my deliverance, and he was stunned. He sat quietly for several minutes and then said, "I was under conviction when I bought this nightclub." I had no clue what Phil meant by conviction. I thought it was a Roman Catholic term.

A couple of nights later, I ran into another guitarist friend, Dan. Dan had played with some famous groups, and we jammed together. He tried to talk me out of quitting. "I'm a Christian too," he said. "But I never felt like I was supposed to quit playing the nightclubs." His final point was that I could do a lot of good for God by remaining in secular music because there were many lost souls I could witness to. I politely disagreed and said my mind was made up. My answer seemed to distress Dan, and he left.

At some point, I sensed I should not say anything else but get rid of everything and go home. I did not fear or try to figure it out. I just went where the path opened up. That day, I started getting things packed in preparation for my last night in the band. When the gig was over the following weekend, I intended to walk away from everything and go unburdened and without any regrets into an unknown future with God in control.

The worst of me had indeed seen the best of God—within the framework of my limited understanding. However, it was merely the prelude to intimacy with the unfathomable and infinite God whose ways are past finding out. The more I knew Him, the more I realized He cannot be measured, contained, and fully defined. He cannot be summed up, boxed up, bottled up, or shut up. Now, as much as I had left Him out, I wanted to let Him in.

LOVE DID

When nothing could fit in my life, Love did
When nothing could make me feel right, Love Did
When emptiness set up a fall
Loneliness built up a wall
Nothing else could tear it down, Love did

Chorus
When sorrow broke my heart in two
Love did what nothing else could do
What I could not give back to You, love did
My soul was held in hate's strong vice
My sins required a sacrifice
When I could not pay the price, Love did

When nothing could show me the way, Love did
When nothing could cheer up my day Love did
The things that I could not forget
Seemed bound within my mind and yet
When I could not erase my past, Love did

Chorus
When sorrow broke my heart in two
Love did what nothing else could do
What I could not give back to You, Love did
My soul was held in hate's strong vice
My sins required a sacrifice
When I could not pay the price, Love did

O Lord, Your love has never failed
You forgave the hands that drove the nails
With every drop of blood that fell
Love Did

CF

CHAPTER 16

HOME AT LAST

I had quit the band and was going home. About noon the day after I told the guys, I was driving down a busy boulevard when Robbie honked and waved at me to pull over. I rolled down my window as he pulled alongside.

"Let's get something to eat," he shouted. "We need to talk about what you said to Freddie."

We went to a restaurant to have lunch and talk. Immediately, Robbie told me he was a Christian. He said he played piano in his dad's church every Sunday morning. I was stunned. I often wondered why he did not party with Ken and me on Sundays but never knew where he spent his time. When I told him what had happened to me, he was very moved. He first told me he believed I was genuinely saved. Then Robbie told me I was doing the right thing in quitting. Before we left, Robbie said he was likewise going to quit someday and that he was just sowing some wild oats—trying to get them out of his system. I was perplexed by that statement, but I did not know exactly how to respond.

The following Monday, I was completely out of the band and had my car loaded. I called David and asked him if he wanted my equipment and that I would sell it cheap. He said yes, so I headed to his apartment. He offered me some cocaine, but I refused. When David gave me the money for my equipment that evening, it was nearly dark. I got in my car and headed for Oklahoma.

It was indeed as if I had been a puppet and God had been pulling the strings. He had led me out of the place where I was stuck and needed guidance and toward the place where He wanted me to be. Now that I was on the road home, I felt He had put me back in the control room. I did not know much about what had happened spiritually. I discovered later that the presence I sensed inside of me was the Holy Spirit.

On the way home, I felt fear and uneasiness about the future trying to intrude. After all, I had no job skills. I had several hundred dollars cash, but it did not provide a significant sense of security. However, I could feel the presence of a force in me that had not been there before. I knew it to be the presence of God. The exuberance that was constantly with me overpowered everything negative. I did not know how or why He did it, but I knew beyond any doubt I had been made one of His people.

I will never forget that night as I drove down Interstate 45 toward home. I looked in my rear-view mirror at the lights of Houston fading away and felt such a great relief. I knew beyond any doubt that I was going in the right direction. It felt so awesome to be free, so weightless, so happy and secure in God. I was through with the music business—that dream I had chased for so long had died. I was completely empty of all desire for anything but my relationship with God. The chains of darkness were very powerful when all I had to struggle against them was my own strength and ability. However, they were no match for the power of God!

I must make it clear that I did not "*get* saved," in the sense that "he got religion," but I *was* saved. I did not "get" anything as one who contracts a sickness or becomes enamored with a philosophical dogma. Someone, God, got me. In His great mercy, grace, and love, He saw me writhing in misery and bondage like a worm on a hook. God offered me something I did not fully understand. All I knew was that the way up had to be the way out.

When I got home, Mama could tell I was different. I gave her my car and took her old car that had a bad transmission. I spent my days praying and reading the Bible. Sometimes, I would take walks down to the lake and sit there praying.

One such day, I was surprised to hear a noise behind me. I turned to see Mama coming down the trail. She said, "Ken called. He said Robbie is dead."

I was shocked. I ran to the house and called Ken back. Robbie and his girlfriend had decided to try out a motorcycle. Ken rode a bike, and Robbie looked up to him like a big brother. But Robbie was not an accomplished rider. He gave the bike too much gas and it jumped out into the stream of rush hour traffic on the Pasadena Freeway. It was the same freeway where I narrowly escaped death when the cement truck nearly hit my stranded car. He and his girlfriend were killed instantly.

One of the things I had procrastinated about was responding to the feeling that I needed to call Robbie. After I had read the Bible more and had grown in knowledge, I remembered what Robbie had said. He said he was going to quit the clubs someday and that he was just sowing some wild oats—trying to get them out of his system. I wanted to tell him, "No Robbie, you are not going to get that lifestyle out of your system, but into your system." I never got that chance.

I thought a lot about it. Why did God save me, a totally corrupt individual and not bring Robbie back to Him? In my reasoning, I didn't deserve a beautiful life of freedom. I was vile and despicable. I deserved to be the one who died. My sins were no doubt piled up much higher than Robbie's. It was a period of deep soul searching.

I questioned whether I was doing enough with the fresh start God had given me.

For a period, a strong sense of unworthiness would come over me. However, I discovered I do not need to *feel* worthy. I just need to know God accepts me. Something is only worth what people will pay for it. God's Son, my Lord and Savior Jesus Christ, paid for me with His life. That is what everyone is worth to God—the life of a sinless King—God's only Son. The sad tragedy is when someone rejects that price and dies in his or her sin.

I reached the conclusion at some point very early in my salvation that I have to do something with this amazing and priceless opportunity. I've been given life when other people had died whom I considered much better than me. I could not and will not let it go to waste. I purposed in my heart and mind that by His grace and strength, I will live for God more committed and surrendered than I had lived for the enemy of all righteousness. As much as I poured out my life for sin, I intend to pour it out much more for God, His perfect will, and to honor His truth.

As one can imagine, there is more to this story. First, it was not long after I got back home that Mama dedicated her heart and life to God. A few weeks later, I took a trip to California to see my dad. He was bedridden with terminal cancer. I witnessed to and prayed with Dad. He said he had made peace with the Lord and died a few weeks later. I had been a Christian for about five years when Mama died of a heart attack. I wish that the first sixty years of her life could have been as peaceful as the last five years.

She wrote the following in her memoir:

"I'll never forget how hard it was all my growing up—and it got even harder after I got married. I just wonder if it will ever be to where I can be free, feel free, from the turmoil of life's rugged way—to cramp us, to where we have to count pennies, to make every penny count for the best places or things."

She is now free, really free, and she feels free. There are no more heartaches in her future. And can you believe it? She and my Dad are both in Heaven having a glorious time together. Neither of them remarried. Their lives would have been very different had they met as Christians. However, I am certain they are best friends in Heaven. No one but God can do such beautiful and wonderful things!

Mama, after she was saved.
Finally, she found peace.

Six months after I was saved, I met the woman who became my wife. Today, I am happily married to the most beautiful and godly woman. We've been best friends and partners in ministry for many years. We have two beautiful and amazing daughters who are completely dedicated to serving God. Both of our daughters are very talented singers, musicians, and songwriters who use their gifts for God's glory. We have four beautiful and talented granddaughters.

They bring great joy to our hearts. It is more wealth than I ever imagined possible when the darkness had me wrapped in its suffocating death grip.

When my first daughter, Leah, was born, beyond the fact that I was a nervous father-to-be, I was apprehensive about her being born with a birth defect. What concerned me was that she would be affected by the amount and type of drugs I had consumed. The day the nurse brought her to me wrapped in the white hospital blanket was an indescribable moment. Her skin was as pink velvet. Her tiny fingers, button nose, and beautiful blue eyes were perfectly formed. To me, it was another indication that God had indeed made me a new creation in Christ.

It sometimes seems too good to be true. For some time after God delivered me, I caught myself wondering if it was going to last. Every day I woke up and realized it was not a dream, I felt overwhelming joy and gratitude to God for His immeasurable love and grace. I can feel that joy and gratitude right now as I write this paragraph.

One final thing—I love my Mama. I wish she were alive so I could tell her I believe she is an amazing woman. I wish I could interview her, hear about her life and all the amazing things she did. Even if no one reads it but my children and grandchildren, I would write a book just about her. I wish I could thank her for taking care of me, feeding, clothing, and providing shelter for me. I wish I could tell her one more time that I love her.

But my soul feasts on the memories of how she changed after giving her heart and soul to God. I remember how she loved flowers. One spring day when riding with my wife and me, she asked us to stop the car. She had spotted some Sweet Williams growing wild beside the highway. Mama got out and climbed a small bank to get a few. She planted them beside the sidewalk to her porch.

I remember her homemade dress and thick hair, gray at the temples, pulled back on the sides, and fastened with large brown celluloid hair combs. I remember the contentment on her face, the twinkle in her eyes and smile crinkles at the corners. I remember how her whole face lit up when we came to visit.

Most of all, I remember her infectious laughter and the countenance of a soul joyful with life. Her spirit was adorned and her heart inundated by the knowledge that God loved her—and likewise her once wayward son, Cedric Hamilton Fisher. Now, she is home at last. And so am I.

My wedding day with my beautiful bride, Cheryl

EPILOGUE

I t has been a painful and poignant experience writing this book. I have had to relive some events and emotions I had pushed far back in my memories. They were so far in the past that I had forgotten most of them. There were times I wept. Other times, I had to stop and thank God for His mercy. However, this testimony is not just about how I messed up my life but how God straightened out the mess.

When I revisit those years of bondage, I realize I am alive right now only by God's grace. At any moment, my heart could have stopped. I could have had a brain aneurysm, died instantly from a gunshot, bled to death while unconscious, stopped my heart with an overdose of drugs, or died in an automobile accident.

God brought me from a miserable, hopeless hell in the temporal realm. It is not something to joke about or revel in. He did not bring me out so I could display my past like a trophy. He delivered me to bring glory and honor to Himself.

After giving my testimony to an atheist, he declared it was merely my will power that had changed me.

I replied, "No I did not say that I changed, I said that I *was* changed, and there is a great difference. I tried to change. I was intelligent enough to realize the lifestyle I was in would end in disaster. I knew I was going to die young. I tried many times, but I could not escape. I could not change. But that moment I yielded my life to God, He changed me in an instant."

That is what happened. I was a vile, evil, tormented, drug addict and alcoholic, filled with hatred and sinfulness. I did not deserve God's love and mercy. I should be in Hell today. But God—and it was all God—delivered and saved me. God was the one who broke my chains.

AFTERWORD

GOD LOVES YOU!

Dear reader,

Perhaps you are not a Christian, in which case you are "lost." It's not that God doesn't know where you are right now. It means you are "lost" to Him or not in His family. The reason is because you have not surrendered your life to Him. In that case, you are in jeopardy of entering eternity "lost." The consequence is to be numbered with Satan, his demons, and every rebellious individual. They will be eternally banished from God's presence. Because God's kingdom is holy and the place where His children will live, His enemies will be sent to a place of torment called Hell.

However, there is great hope in a short story I want to share with you. Because of His love, God made a way for you to be in His family and avoid Hell. He sent His only Son, Jesus, to pay the penalty of your sin. Jesus was tried, falsely convicted, and sentenced to die. After beating Him almost to death, Romans soldiers executed Him by nailing Him to a cross where He died a slow and excruciating death. Three days later, God raised Him from the dead.

Now Jesus sits on the right side of God His Father waiting to return to Earth. He will come with vengeance upon the wicked and rebellious human race and cast Satan and his minions into the abyss. No one knows when this event will happen. When it occurs, the offer to become a child of God will be withdrawn.

Because Jesus paid the penalty for your sin, you have an opportunity to join God's family. All you must do to accept what

Jesus did is to fully surrender to God, confess that Christ Jesus is both Lord and Savior, and believe in your heart that God raised Him from the dead. If you sincerely mean it, the Lord will come into your heart, and you will begin a relationship with God. Your life will show evidence of this relationship as He puts a desire in you to reject your old ways and live according to His Word. God's Holy Spirit will come inside of you to assist you in living godly and obeying God.

Your enemy, Satan, may whisper in your spirit to consider what you are giving up. For me, I knew that sin's misery and eternal penalty is not worth the temporary pleasure it may provide. I know most of the excuses for not surrendering to God because I used many of them myself. Please realize that life here is very short compared to eternity. We only have a certain span to surrender to God. Who knows if today is your last day on Earth?

You may think, "But I'm not *that* bad," or, "I'm *too* bad for God to save me." No one is so bad that God cannot save him or so good he does not need to be saved!

If you decide to surrender to God, you will want to meet with a group of true believers. There are denominations and many churches, but there is only one true church—the Body of Jesus Christ. Thus, there is no telling where you will find true Christians meeting. It may be in a house where a few are gathered, in a storefront building, in a prison, or a beautiful edifice. The primary thing is to go where there are believers who have put their trust in the Lord Jesus Christ and believe that the Bible is His Word.

You also should depend on God more than people. This does not mean you should reject leadership. Please don't be unwilling or afraid to be discipled by leaders, but make certain they are godly leaders. No one is perfect, but you will recognize the ones who are godly.

As your walk with the Lord grows, it is important that you develop a daily routine of praying and reading His Word. If you do not invest yourself in prayer and the study of God's Word, you will be susceptible to deception, weakness, and defeat.

You should know one more thing. You came to God during a time of great apostasy in Christianity. I personally believe it is the final apostasy before the coming of Jesus Christ. You may wonder, "What is an apostasy?" It is departure from true faith as presented in God's Word. Many professing Christians have become apostate today. They have added to and altered the true Gospel to support their defection. Therefore, you might visit a church service where you feel uncomfortable. The Holy Spirit may reveal that there is no sincerity for God or His truth or that something else is very wrong. You need to leave that place as soon as possible.

Please remember this. People may fail you, let you down, betray you, reject you, or hurt you, but God never will. Don't become bitter. Do not blame God for what people do. And don't blame Christ Jesus—He died for you.

Finally, remember this: the Bible tells us to put on the armor of God (Ephesians 6:11-19), and with it, we will be able to stand against evil, walk in righteousness and victory, and bring this message of peace and salvation to others.

In His will, for His cause,

Cedric H. Fisher

Behold, I stand at the door, and knock: if
any man hear my voice, and open the door,
I will come in to him, and will sup with
him, and he with me. (Revelation 3:20)

AN AFTERWORD
FROM CHERYL

He walked onto the stage, guitar in hand, and as he did, a hush seemed to fill the room. Then he began to sing! His face was shining with the light of the Glory of God, and even though we didn't know his story, we knew he had surely had a powerful experience with God.

I leaned over to my friend sitting beside me and said, "I'm going to marry that man."

My friend laughed at me and said, "You don't even know him."

I replied, "I know, but I'm going to marry him anyway." And . . . I did!

After 38 years of marriage, two children, and four grandchildren, I can truthfully say that the same anointing we felt in that room the first time I ever met my husband is still present in his life.

We have been together almost every day of our married lives. That's a lot of days together. I have watched my husband, who has also been my pastor, for nearly all those 38 years, day in and day out, and I have never seen him falter in his walk with Christ. We've been through some very difficult times, and I have watched the faith of this man grow and stand strong. His love and desire for God is relentless. He is a mighty and faithful prayer warrior and a speaker of truth. If I could sum it up, I would simply say, He is a genuine man of God.

When he was asked to write this book, I know he was a bit hesitant. He's never been one to glorify his testimony and is always cautious to not put the focus on himself but to give the glory to God alone. However, it never fails to bring tears to my eyes when I hear him speak of how God took an angry, hopeless young man whose life consisted of drugs, alcohol, deep pain, hatred, and misery and instantly set him free. Satan tried so many times to take his life and destroy him, but God saw the heart of someone who desperately needed to be loved.

I look at my husband and cannot imagine the person he was before Christ. I am so thankful for a God who can take someone so entrenched in the darkness and bring him into His marvelous light. It is our prayer that this book has encouraged you to pray for your sons, your daughters, and

Cheryl and Cedric today

your friends who may be bound in chains of destruction. If God can reach down into a nightclub and speak to an angry young man's heart and bring him out of bondage, He can do the same for anyone. Only Christ can set the captive free.

Cheryl Fisher

TOPICAL BOOKLETS BY CEDRIC FISHER

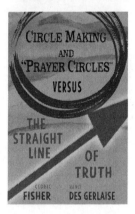

The Unacknowledged War and the Wearing Down of the Saints
Faith Under Fire: Are you Growing in It or Fleeing From It?
IF It is of God: Answering the Questions about IF: Gathering
Circle Making and "Prayer Circles" Versus the Straight Line of Truth

These booklets are published by Lighthouse Trails and are available at www.lighthousetrails.com. They are 10-18 pages long and sell for $1.95 each.

OTHER MEANINGFUL BIOGRAPHIES
BY LIGHTHOUSE TRAILS

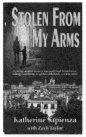

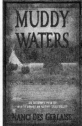

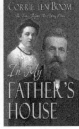
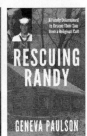

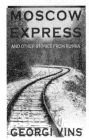
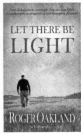

Visit the Lighthouse
Trails website for a
complete listing of all
our books, DVDs,
CDs, and more.
Resources you can trust!
www.lighthousetrails.com

To order additional copies of:
Chains Couldn't Hold Me
Send $14.95 per book plus shipping
($3.95 for 1 book, $6.00 flat rate for all other quantities) to:
Lighthouse Trails Publishing
P.O. Box 908
Eureka, Montana 59917

You may also order online at:
www.lighthousetrails.com
or
Call our toll free number:
866/876-3910
[ORDER LINE]
E-mail: sales@lighthousetrails.com.
For all other calls: 406/889-3610
Fax: 406/889-3633

Chains Couldn't Hold Me, as well as all books by Lighthouse Trails Publishing, can be ordered directly from Lighthouse Trails or through all major outlet stores, bookstores, online bookstores, and Christian bookstores.

Bookstores may order through
Ingram, Spring Arbor, Anchor
or directly through Lighthouse Trails.
Libraries may order through Baker & Taylor.

Quantity discounts available for most of our books.
International orders may be placed either online,
through e-mail or by faxing or writing.

You may visit the author's website at:
http://www.truthkeepers.com.